SHEPHERD OF SOULS

Fr. Cleopa in his sheepskin coat.

Shepherd of Souls

The Life and Teachings of Elder Cleopa,
Master of Inner Prayer and Spiritual Father
of Romania (1912–1998)

By Archimandrite Ioanichie Balan

ST. HERMAN OF ALASKA BROTHERHOOD
2000

Copyright 2000 by the
St. Herman of Alaska Brotherhood

First Printing

Address all correspondence to:
St. Herman of Alaska Brotherhood
P. O. Box 70
Platina, California 96076

Front cover: The peaceful gaze of inward stillness: Elder Cleopa in his last years.

Back cover: Fr. Cleopa revisiting the sheepfold of Sihastria Monastery, Romania.

Library of Congress Cataloging in Publication Data
Ioanichie (Balan), Archimandrite.
   Shepherd of souls: the life of Elder Cleopa, master of inner prayer and spiritual father of Romania (1912–1998).
   Translated from the Romanian.
Library of Congress Catalogue Number: 00-109555
ISBN 1-887904-04-2

Contents

Voronets Monastery in Moldavia, frescoed on the outside in the late sixteenth century. Scene of the Last Judgment. A Romanian man in traditional dress.

INTRODUCTION

WHENEVER I ponder on the fact that I met Elder Cleopa personally—not just once but many times—I realize that I encountered a man who knew God and who lived in Paradise even while here on earth. I met someone who had received a spiritual wholeness by growing up in a traditional Orthodox society. This wholeness was transmitted to his developing soul not only through the religious life of the Romanian people but through all aspects of village life. Thus, the shepherd boy grew and developed with an integrity rarely seen in the contemporary world.

Fr. Cleopa grew up in a small Romanian village in northern Moldavia. Romania's deep Christian roots were planted nearly two thousand years ago when the Apostle Andrew evangelized this Balkan country. The region of Bucovina where he was raised is Romania's most pious region. Days are numbered according to the feasts and fasts. Even today, if you drive through his village on a feast day, you will see families sitting on benches outside their front gates, talking with their neighbors while the children play nearby. No one will be working that day. There is a Romanian saying that eternity was born in the village.

With their occupation of tending the sheep and tilling the land, Fr. Cleopa's family was the cause of his deep connection with the earth and his harmony with all nature. He was not a product of modern society, nor was his soul deformed by the constant bombardment of television and computers.

Rather, his soul was allowed to blossom, as his mind and thoughts were impressed with images of beauty and holiness in the silence of nature. The powers of his soul, such as the ability to observe how God works in His creation, and the humility of wisdom, were not distorted.

The result of this formation was an uncluttered and vibrant soul fertile to apprehend the deep mysteries of God. The raising of the heart and mind to God in prayer, as well as the virtue of patiently "waiting on the Lord," were natural to him. Later, when he began to read the Holy Fathers, there was nothing to hinder their teachings from taking root in his heart, mind, and will. He was blessed with an incredible memory, so that whatever he read was imprinted like a "finger writing upon wax." His early years in the monastery he spent "gathering" in the sheepfold—that is, reading and absorbing potent spiritual books that would later bear fruit a hundredfold for the Romanian people. God called him at an early age to tend a rational flock, and for over fifty years he was a beacon to whom thousands flocked for his wisdom and counsel. I was one of them.

The first time I was blessed to meet Fr. Cleopa was April of 1991, when he was 79 years old. I had heard of Fr. Cleopa from my spiritual father even in 1988, before the communist dictatorship had fallen, when Romania was still a closed country. Despite the repression behind the Iron Curtain, word of the Elder had reached the West, and I already knew that he was a renowned spiritual father at Sihastria Monastery, whom the communists were afraid to silence because of his great popularity. I was on pilgrimage to Romania. Fr. Ioanichie Balan of Sihastria, a spiritual son of the Elder and the author of this biography, was our host. I had come with another American nun who was intent on translating into English another of Fr.

Ioanichie's books, *Romanian Patericon,* although she did not yet know the Romanian language.

Fr. Cleopa had been at Sihastria Monastery uninterruptedly since 1964, receiving pilgrims daily at his "lower cell." To reach his cell, one must first enter the monastery through the front gate. Toward the back of the monastery near the lower guesthouse, there is a steep staircase leading up and away from the main part of the monastery, which turns into a narrow path. This path leads to a wooden cell with a row of benches outside, facing the cell. Usually there would be many people sitting there and quietly waiting, in expectation, for Fr. Cleopa to come out onto the verandah and speak to them. There is now an awning, but that is a recent addition. Before, if it was raining, pilgrims and visitors would be sitting under their umbrellas.

When Fr. Cleopa would come out accompanied by a cell-attendant, the faithful would rush forward to kiss his hand out of love and respect and to receive his fatherly blessing. He then would give a "profitable word" (as the Romanians say) from his vast wealth of experience. It could be a story of a saint or from the Scriptures or from his own life. The pilgrims also asked him many questions. These sessions with the Elder continued even during the time of church services. When the church bells rang at a given part of the service, everyone would stop to cross themselves. After he had finished speaking, the people would approach him again to receive his blessing and, at this time, many would hand him a list of the names of their close ones to be prayed for.

During all my stays at Sihastria Monastery I was able to participate in this central activity of the monastery's life—going up to see Fr. Cleopa. His presence drew hundreds of people every day. The monks received all in true Christian love and hospitality—feeding and housing everyone.

Fr. Cleopa in his younger days.

Fr. Cleopa in later years.

I was drinking at a wellspring of grace. I was transported into the otherworldliness of Christ's presence by being there in the monastery and in the Elder's presence. I loved this deeply Christian culture—the monasteries, the monks and nuns, the villages, the horses and carts, the haying season, the sheep-folds—eternity in a Christian culture. My soul was thriving and my spirit soared. My first impulse was to leave the modern Western world behind forever, stay there and sit at the feet of Fr. Cleopa and the other holy Elders I had met.

But I realized that God had given me the opportunity to meet Fr. Cleopa and the Elders for another reason: to bring something of what I had experienced back with me to America. Our land also needs to be given a portion of the spiritual nourishment that comes through meeting a spiritual hero like Fr. Cleopa. It is our desire in presenting Fr. Cleopa's Life* that, like honey bees gathering nectar, we will extract the essence of the genuine Christian struggle which lies hidden within the flower of his life, so that we too may follow the path of holiness in the country God has placed us.

Mother Nina
St. Nilus Island, Alaska
May 7(20), 2000
Feast of St. Nilus of Sora

* In this English translation of Elder Cleopa's Life, all footnotes are by the translator and editor.

PART I

THE LIFE OF ELDER CLEOPA OF SIHASTRIA

Children in traditional dress from Bucovina, the region where
Fr. Cleopa was raised.

I

Childhood

THE man who would one day become the renowned guide of souls, Elder Cleopa, was born into this world as Constantine Ilie on April 10, 1912, in a rural village of Botosani County in Romania. Constantine's father, Alexander, was from a line of shepherds from the region of Sibiu in Transylvania (northwestern Romania). One of his ancestors moved to Moldavia in the eighteenth century to escape religious persecution. Constantine's mother, Anna, was also from an agricultural family. In those days life flowed smoothly like sweet water from an abundant spring, for such was the inheritance the Romanians had received from their Christian ancestors. Traditional life in Romania was rooted in its faith, which it had received originally from the Apostle Andrew, and in a simple existence centered on working the land. The flow of life received its impulse from the cycle of church services. Blessings from the local priest were received before projects were undertaken, so that earthly blessings would follow.

As a baby Constantine was sickly; he hardly ate anything, and cried incessantly day and night. Taking the advice of the old women of the village, Anna brought her son to the renowned spiritual father Conon Gavrilescu of Cozancea Skete, who was known as a great exorcist and had healed many of the sick through prayer.

"What do I do, Father? For some time my child has refused to eat and cries without stop. I am afraid he will die," pleaded the mother.

"Do you know what you must do?" replied the Elder. "Dedicate him to the Mother of the Lord!"

"How do I present him to the Mother of the Lord?"

"This is how," he said. "Take the baby in your arms and lay him down in front of the icon of the Mother of the Lord in church and say, 'Mother of God, I present you with this child who is sick. Do what you will with him in order to make him healthy.'"

The weeping mother then went into the church, made three prostrations before the icon of the Mother of God, fell on her knees, and made her plea. Finishing her prayer, Anna passed under the icon three times.* Fr. Conon then served the child Holy Communion and read the prayer for health. This resulted in a miraculous intercession by the Mother of God— the infant was soon healthy and became an energetic child.

Alexander Ilie was the father of ten children, the fifth of whom was Constantine. His land consisted of 75 acres, on which he raised over 20 head of cattle and tended 150 sheep. He was one of the more prosperous ranchers in the area. On every feast day he took his family to the church of God. His character was firm and manly, but in it there also existed sensitivity and mercifulness, which he directed to the poor and needy through the giving of alms.

Anna Ilie was a devout woman of prayer who loved her children dearly. She was short in stature, and although she never learned to read, she possessed a remarkable memory. It was this gift of memory which Elder Cleopa inherited from his mother that would be his distinguishing characteristic as a great spiritual father and orator. The depth of Anna's character and spiritual life grew out of the many hardships she faced in

* In Romania it is an act of piety to pass on your knees under an icon of the Mother of God.

life. Her greatest sorrow was that almost all her children died young.* She wept often not only from the many sorrows that visited her, but even more from contrition of heart and thanksgiving toward God. She was able to transmit to her children a highly refined sense of the sacred and a love for the holy things of God. Five of her children dedicated their lives wholly to Christ in the monastic life.

Early in the morning, before school, Anna would prepare the children and in her tender care would tell them to eat something or take something to eat on the way. Her husband would then reprove her, "No! Let them be. They won't die." And so, the four brothers—Michael, Basil, George, and Constantine—would walk to school where they would first eat a piece of holy bread and, only then, have breakfast. At home Alexander would not allow the boys to eat in the morning until they had prayed for an hour. Wishing to emulate the ascetic heroism of the saints, the boys themselves loved to fast and were known at school for giving their lunches to others. The eldest, Michael, who was the first to become a monk, took on the daily practice of fasting until he had read the entire Psalter. Even if it was not a time appointed by the Church for fasting, Alexander would say to his boys, "Let's not eat now. Wait until

* Alexander and Anna's children were Maria (born 1903), Basil (1905), George (1907), Profira (1910), Constantine (1912), Catherine (1914), Michael (1917), Hareta (1920), and two more children who died in infancy. Maria married in her native village and gave birth to a girl. Her whole family died at a young age. Basil and George entered Sihastria Monastery and they both died young. Profira never married. She bore the burden of the family, working in the fields and taking care of her little brothers and sisters. One day, while weeding in the fields, she felt sick and asked Constantine to read the Psalter for her. While he read, she gave her soul into God's hands. Catherine entered Old Agapia Monastery but later moved to Agafton Monastery, where she died at a young age. Michael entered Durau Monastery in 1934 and later moved to Cozancea Skete, where he reposed in 1940. Hareta lived at home and died at a young age.

A typical village house in the region where Fr. Cleopa was raised.

Romanian peasants working the land.

you come home at noon. You aren't pigs that need to be fed in the morning."

Considering his healing as a small child, it is not surprising that Constantine developed a great devotion to the Mother of God at an early age. By the time he was eleven years old, he could sing the Akathist Hymn by heart. He would later tell the story of how he learned this ancient and poetic prayer: "When I shucked corn in the field I would hide the prayer book under the husks until Father would come with the horse-cart. During this time I would learn one more ikos and one more kontakion. And, lo and behold, I learned the entire Akathist to the Mother of God."

In the house of Alexander and Anna Ilie there was one room covered with icons which was like a small chapel. The family would rise early in the morning to pray together there. It was in this room that the four future monks first developed their desire for the ascetic life. In this spiritually nurturing environment the boys spent their childhood, working the fields and tending the animals. Constantine was naturally inclined to avoid worldly distractions. His mother would say that when he was returning home from tending the sheep, he would purposely avoid going through the village if there was a wedding or a party.

Within these wholesome surroundings the boys did not, however, pass their youth without engaging in a little mischievous activity. Elder Cleopa was known to reminisce about one particular incident: "When I was little and coming home from school, I passed through the village and saw some boys throwing rocks at a house with a red metal roof. I, too, joined in and began throwing rocks. Our teacher heard about it and took us all aside and slapped us. Now I thank him because he did a good thing for me, and I pray for him."

2

Cozancea Skete

In a humble cell in the nearby woods there lived the desert-dweller and monk Paisius Olaru. This cell was in the vicinity of Cozancea Skete, located about five kilometers from the village. Every summer Alexander would graze his sheep on the hills and meadows near the skete. When the boys came of age, he gave the care of the sheep into the hands of the three brothers—Basil, George and Constantine—all of whom had roamed these hills since their earliest childhood.

Fr. Paisius was born in Botosani County in 1897. At the age of twenty-five he entered Cozancea Skete, where he labored in the ascetic life for the next twenty-six years, praising God day and night and comforting many souls. From the time that Constantine was a little boy, he and his brothers would visit Fr. Paisius and help the monks do chores around the skete, assisting the older monks and singing on the cliros.

So it was ordained by God that these young shoots would be spiritually formed to one day become spiritual giants of contemporary monasticism. Whenever the youths were troubled in soul or in a time of temptation, they would run to Fr. Paisius and ask him for a profitable word. The monk would counsel them to keep silence, to pray the Jesus Prayer, to make daily prostrations, and, after milking the sheep at night, to read the Psalter and sing the Akathist to the Mother of God. In their youthful zeal the brothers would faithfully fulfill all that their spiritual father commanded. Because of their obedience, the enemy would tempt them more and more, being unable to bear being vanquished by some children who banished him with the power of prayer.

Hieroschema-monk Paisius Olaru with spiritual daughters.

At night the brothers would gather to pray. At certain times sounds could be heard from the attic, which disturbed their prayer. Constantine, the youngest, would stop and ask his brothers, "Do you hear that?" But the eldest of the brothers, Basil, would quickly reprove him, "Be quiet! Don't pay any attention to it. That's the worst he can do."

One night they were gathered around the fire at the sheepfold reading the Psalter. Suddenly they saw a strange bird swoop down into their midst. Being more exuberant, the young Constantine stopped reading and exclaimed, "Look what a beautiful bird it is!"

"Be quiet! Pray and don't say anything more!" Basil admonished him.

While Constantine was staring at the bird it suddenly threw itself into the fire, making a loud noise, scattering all the coals and catching the sheepfold on fire. Many of the sheep died and only with great difficulty were they able to put out the fire and gather the frightened sheep. After this they ran to their Elder, Fr. Paisius, and reported to him this demonic temptation. The Elder sprinkled the sheep and the fold with holy water and encouraged the brothers not to be afraid, because the devil is ultimately bound by Christ and does not have the power to kill men.

3
Temptations of Youth

By the early 1920s, to the north of Romania, the government of the great Orthodox nation of Russia had been overthrown by the violent Bolshevik Revolution, and Russia was now in the hands of the communists. Mass graves were being filled with the bodies of confessing bishops, priests, monks,

Two young Romanian shepherds.

nuns, and others who were considered "enemies of the people." In Romania the Communist Party had just been formed (1921), and in 1930 the tyrannical dictator Carol II seized the throne from the rightful King Michael, who was still a minor. Romania found itself caught between the two strongest totalitarian powers in Europe—Germany and the Soviet Union. Both were greedy for its natural resources and for political control of the Balkans. Despite these political rumblings, life in rural Moldavia continued on calmly and peacefully.*

The innocence of youth was not destroyed in Constantine and his brothers, as it is in so many during their teen-age years. The boys maintained their zeal for God and kept their ascetic edge sharpened as a sword ready for battle.

As the Ilie boys grew into young men, their mother Anna, following her maternal instincts, desired to have them married. Anna would bring girls from the village to the evening corn-husking parties in the hope that one of them would fall in love with one of her boys. This plan backfired, as the young men used the opportunity to speak to the young women about the saints. One young woman became so inspired that she soon left home and went to a convent, where others shortly followed after her. The young Constantine, especially, showed a special talent for speaking words of spiritual edification and displayed a pastoral heart in the care for the salvation of souls. Seeing her hopes for future marriages dashed, Anna would sob. She feared that she would soon lose all her boys to the monastic life.

In 1925, according to an old Romanian custom, the young people from the village hired two fiddlers to play at the Ilie house. The music was being played and all were singing

---

* See "A Brief Outline of Romanian History" in *The Orthodox Word* no. 155 (1990), pp. 327–46.

A village dance in Romania.

and dancing, as Romanians love to do. Anna was excited, seeing another opportunity for romance to develop between one of the village girls and one of her sons. At one point George saw that the icon of the Mother of God began to weep. Understanding the meaning of this, the three brothers left the house and hid. Noticing their sudden absence, Anna went looking everywhere for them. Upset, she finally found them, "Why do you shame us in front of the village?" she asked. "Come and dance." George quickly and secretly punched a hole in his boot with his knife and replied, "Mama, how can I come and dance when I have a hole in my boots?"

That evening Anna and Alexander realized that their sons had chosen another path in life, and they resolved to leave them to serve Christ alone.

4
Young Ascetics

Now in their early twenties, Basil and George began to prepare earnestly for the monastic life. They would rise at midnight to chant Matins and read the Psalter. They would also wake up Constantine, who was at this time fifteen years old. Constantine resented being deprived of his sleep. His oldest sister, Maria, had entered the Army of the Lord,* and she persuaded Constantine, "You should also enter the Army of the Lord, because you have the gift of speaking, and it isn't nearly as difficult as the monastic life." He agreed, and on the following night, when his brothers woke him up at midnight for prayer, he told them not to wake him up anymore because he was not going to be a monk. He went back to bed and slept without any care.

That night Anna was still up working. Coming back from the well with two buckets of water, she saw in Constantine's room a big dog which was sitting on his chest and licking his cheek. She called out, "Basil, come quickly, because Constantine is being eaten by a dog!" Constantine awoke just in time to see the tail of a big black dog, which then disappeared. Basil told him, "That was the devil, who is glad that you are no longer going to the monastery!" From that moment on, Constantine no longer doubted whether he wanted to be a monk. Each night he arose for prayer so that he would not be subject to demonic attack through his slothfulness.

In 1927 George left home at the age of twenty-five to become a disciple of the desert-dweller Paisius at Cozancea Skete.

---

* Founded in 1927, the Army of the Lord was a group of Orthodox Christians dedicated to bringing about spiritual revival among the Romanian people through preaching and composing religious songs.

There he lived in obedience, working in the garden, singing on the cliros, practicing the Jesus Prayer, and eating only once a day.

Having embarked on the monastic way of life, George quickly fell into temptation. Giving heed to trusting his own thoughts, he entered the cell of the Elder and left a note which read, "Forgive me, Fr. Paisius, I have gone into the woods to repent for five days."

In the evening the Elder read the note and discerned the cunning of the enemy: "This is a temptation of the devil, and it will not be beneficial to Br. George because he departed without a blessing." Just after midnight he heard a knock on his door and a voice which said, "Bless, Fr. Paisius, and forgive me a sinner."

"Who are you?" the Elder asked.

"Br. George, the sinner."

"How is that possible? Br. George went into the woods for five days in order to repent."

"Forgive me, Fr. Paisius. I have sinned."

"May God forgive you, Br. George. Come on in and tell me what happened."

"For a long time I had wanted to pray alone for a few days in the woods, Fr. Paisius. So I took the Horologion, the Psalter, a few candles, and matches, and I hid in the woods in a den. I began to make prostrations there and to pray with tears. At midnight I heard a voice that said, 'What are you doing here?' I turned around and saw a hideous creature of a fearful appearance. It was the enemy. Then he said to me, 'Why did you leave without a blessing?' Then, overwhelmed with great fear, I took the Horologion and ran! Please, Fr. Paisius, forgive me a sinner and receive me back."

From that day on, Br. George never did anything without a blessing.

Toward the end of 1927 George sought to enter Sihastria

Skete. Knowing the zeal of the young struggler's soul, the Abbot of Sihastria put him to the test before accepting him into the brotherhood. For three days he had George stay outside the gate, carrying a sack of dirt on his back and repeating Psalm 50 ten times consecutively. When he finished, he would take a short rest and then repeat the process. At the end of three days the Abbot said to him, "Br. George, how do you like monasticism? Monastic life is difficult. You have to fast, pray, do what you are commanded, and carry on your back the labor of a monk with love until death."

"Forgive me, a sinner. With the help of God I will fulfill, according to my weak strength, all that is ordained for me to do."

Br. George was then accepted into the monastery and given the obedience of caring for the cattle.

5
Basil and Constantine Leave Home

Shortly after the feast of St. Nicholas, in the winter of 1929, Basil and Constantine made the resolution to leave home and give their lives to Christ in the monastic life. They set their sights on the Sihastria Monastery. The monastery's name is derived from the Greek *hesychia,* which means silence.

After they received the blessing of their village priest, they told their parents of their intention. Seeing the last of her boys leave home, the mother's heart was rent in twain. In the flood of her tears, Alexander admonished her with these words, "Let them go! Why didn't we think like them when we were their age? Behold, tomorrow we go to the Lord, and what does this earthly life avail?"

Each brother took with him only a shoulder bag containing a small quantity of clothes, the Holy Bible, the *Lives of*

Saints, the Horologion, the Psalter. They also took two icons: one of the Mother of God which had wept in their home,* and another of St. George, the patron of their brother, who had already reached the calm harbor of monastic life.

Saying a final prayer before departing on their lifelong journey, the brothers were accompanied by their parents to the outskirts of the village. Seeing the painful state of their loving parents at this most fateful parting, Basil broke out into song with a verse from the Akathist to the Savior: "Warrior-Chieftain and Lord, vanquisher of hell, I Thy creature and servant offer Thee songs of praise, for Thou hast delivered me from eternal death. But as Thou hast unutterable lovingkindness, free me from every danger as I cry: Jesus, Son of God, have mercy on me!" Thus they crossed themselves, kissed their parents' hands, and departed toward Cozancea Skete. At this moment both Alexander and Anna broke down and cried.

6
A New Life

Taking leave of their grieving parents, Basil and Constantine followed the familiar trail that led to Fr. Paisius' cell near Cozancea Skete. This time, however, they were embarking on the first steps of a new life. The path would undoubtedly be rocky but at the same time would offer the young men a way of life that could fulfill their idealistic dreams of serving God without compromise.

There to meet them at Cozancea Skete was Br. George, who was visiting Fr. Paisius. After resting for the evening and hearing many stories about the desert-dwellers who lived in the

---

* This icon was later given as a blessing to a family in the Neamts region, where it is to this day.

Neamts Mountains, the trio of brethren departed to Suceava to venerate the relics of St. John the New.* The pilgrims then made their way to the famous Neamts Monastery to venerate the wonder-working icon of the Mother of God, under whose protection are gathered all the monasteries in the land of Moldavia. From Neamts the brothers entered the Secu Valley and paid their respects to the founder of Secu Monastery, Nestor Ureche. They prayed on the very ground where the great light of contemporary monasticism, St. Paisius Velichkovsky, had lived in oneness of soul with his community of five hundred monks.

As they passed through those blessed mountains—where hundreds of hermits had lived God-pleasing lives in silence, far from the praise of men—they all gave glory to God. They were filled with the bright hope that they too would be blessed by the Mother of God to follow in their footsteps. Finally they reached their destination: the desert skete of Sihastria.

7
A Brief History of Sihastria Skete

The Sihastria Skete lies in a valley in the foothills of the Carpathian Mountains. Monastic life was founded there in 1655 by the holy hesychast Athanasius together with one disciple. The skete was renewed in 1734 by Bishop Gideon, who constructed a wooden church, a group of cells, and a bell-tower. These were burned to the ground by the Turks in 1821.

---

* St. John the New was martyred for his faith by the idol-worshipping Tatars in Cetata Alba (Belgorod) in 1330. His relics were brought to Romania for the first time six hundred years ago and have been in the city of Suceava since the seventeenth century. He is known as the protector of Moldavia and his relics are a site of pilgrimage for Romanians, especially on his feast day, June 24.

The church in Suceava where rest the relics of St. John the New.

Neamts Monastery.

The Romanian countryside.

The miracle-working icon of the Mother of God at Neamts Monastery.

St. Paisius Velichkovksy of Neamts.

Sihastria Monastery as it appears today.

In 1824 the church was rebuilt by Metropolitan Benjamin Costache.* The area of land surrounding the skete was secularized between 1861 and 1863, during which time the skete became nearly desolate.

In 1884 a lumber mill was constructed in the vicinity of the skete, forcing the remaining monks to seek refuge deeper in the mountains. One monk, Jonathan, was left to take care of the skete church, and he stayed at his post for twenty-five years. Liturgy was served once a year on September 8, the patronal feast day of the Nativity of the Mother of God.

---

* Metropolitan Benjamin Costache, called "the heir of Elder Paisius' divine zeal," himself served at St. Paisius' funeral. As the head of the Moldavian Church from 1803 to 1842, he built churches and schools, and printed Patristic literature and textbooks for students. He is remembered for his great influence in bringing about a Paisian revival and for his unequivocal love for all men.

8

Archimandrite Ioanichie Moroi— Renewer of Sihastria Skete

In the year 1890 the future Archimandrite Ioanichie Moroi went on a pilgrimage to the Lord's Sepulchre in Jerusalem and then continued west to the monastic republic of Mt. Athos. Here he made the decision to leave his family and follow Christ in the monastic state, remaining in a Romanian kellion on the Holy Mountain for ten years. In 1900 he returned to Romania, where he entered Neamts Monastery with the obedience of sacristan.

Fr. Cleopa would later tell the following story about Fr. Ioanichie, which took place at Neamts:

"In the year 1907 an old monk died, who was over ninety years old. His name was Dometian. He did not hear well, and when he would come to the services in the church he would stand near the tomb of St. Paisius [Velichkovsky], which is found in the big church to this day. Very often he would weep because he could not hear the services in church. His cell was far from the church. One day Fr. Ioanichie heard the news that Monk Dometian the Deaf had died and that some of the monks had found him dead on his knees in front of the holy icons and had then told the Abbot. The Abbot told the great ecclesiarch to take care of everything. The ecclesiarch sent a few monks to bring him to the church, because such is the order for monks. If he [the deceased] is a priest, he must stay in the church and the monks read the Psalter near his coffin for three days and nights. When the monks went to bring him into the church, they saw that he was very poor, not having anything but the old and torn garments in which

Lacu Skete on Mt. Athos: a Romanian skete that Fr. Ioanichie
Moroi would have visited.

A contemporary Romanian hermit on Mt. Athos:
Fr. Ilia of St. Anne's Skete.

Abbot Ioanichie Moroi.

he was clothed. The monks brought clothes and dressed him, put him on the bier, and brought him into the church, placing him in the exonarthex. The ecclesiarch brought the great schema, with which the dead are covered until the burial, and put it over him. Then, since it was evening and the ecclesiarch knew that the monk Ioanichie read the Psalter a lot, he said to him, 'Ioanichie, I know that you do not sleep and you read the Psalter until Matins. Therefore, until I arrange for the others to come here, you read.' Fr. Ioanichie replied, 'Bless to read!' and he remained in the exonarthex so as to read the Psalter.

"Only he and the dead one remained. At nine in the evening the reposed monk Dometian, lying in his coffin, raised his leg up. Fr. Ioanichie went and pressed down on the knee, returning the dead monk's leg to its place, and continued to read the Psalter. However, an hour later the monk raised up his other leg. Fr. Ioanichie was then frightened and asked the dead monk, 'Fr. Dometian, have you resurrected? If you have resurrected, tell me, because I am commemorating you as dead.' He did not hear any response. Believing that Fr. Dometian had resurrected and could not speak because his mouth was covered by his kamilavka, Fr. Ioanichie untied the ends of the kamilavka, uncovered his face, and again asked him, 'Fr. Dometian, are you alive?' And the Elder Dometian opened wide his mouth and kept it open for a quarter of an hour. Then out of his mouth came a very pleasant fragrance which filled the church, and because the doors of the church were open, the sweet smell spread throughout all the monastery. Nevertheless, Fr. Ioanichie went on reading the Psalter and, after an hour, went to receive a blessing to beat the semantron for the beginning of Matins. At 11:00 P.M., when the monks began to come to church, they sensed that good fragrance and wondered about its origin. Fr. Ioanichie, after beating the semantron and ringing the bells for Matins, came to church, and everyone asked him if knew anything about this wonderful fragrance. He told them that he knew and that after the service he would tell them more. Thus, after the service of Matins ended at two in the morning, everyone being gathered in the church, he told them that the fragrance came out of the mouth of Dometian, who was dead, as well as everything that had happened while he was reading the Psalter.

"The monks, hearing this, gave glory to God, and they all brought their Psalters from their cells and gathered near the coffin of Fr. Dometian. After they finished they no longer said, 'God forgive you, Fr. Dometian' as is customary, but 'Holy Fr. Dometian, pray to God for us.' When Fr. Dometian had been buried and his grave sealed, again a sweet aroma issued forth from his blessed mouth, and all wept and glorified God Who exalts the humble and those disdained in this world."*

In 1909 the lumber mill was closed at Sihastria and Schema-monk Ioanichie was ordained a priest and selected as abbot to renew the skete. Thus Sihastria was reborn, having as its leader a monk who—like the monk responsible for the monastic revival in the eighteenth and nineteenth centuries in Romania and Russia, St. Paisius Velichkovsky—had been formed on Mt. Athos.

For twenty years Fr. Ioanichie served the Liturgy daily as the only priest in the skete. Daily life was modeled after the Athonite standard. Matins was held at midnight, followed by the Liturgy and the complete cycle of services. The Abbot would not allow the services to begin until all the brothers

---

* From *Urcus Spre Inviere* by Archimandrite Cleopa Ilie (Trinitas, 1992), pp. 395–97.

were present in church. Confession was given weekly and the brothers received Communion every thirty to forty days, as was the custom, according to each one's zeal. On Monday, Wednesday, and Friday one meal was served after 3:00 P.M., while on the other days two meals were served with dairy products.

Each monk was obliged to fulfill his cell-rule which consisted of three hundred prostrations, six hundred bows, and daily reading from the Psalter. Those who did not fulfill their cell-rule were not allowed to eat that day. No one was allowed to receive relatives into his cell, possess money of his own, or to speak on worldly topics. Each monk's primary focus was the continual practice of the Jesus Prayer, through which thoughts are cleansed and the heart is purified.

Fr. Ioanichie led the brothers by his own exemplary and genuine cross-bearing life of self-renunciation. Fr. Cleopa would later recall about his predecessor: "Because he would serve the Liturgy daily, he would not eat anything from Monday through Friday, being satisfied only with Holy Communion and prosphora. During the five days the Abbot would come to trapeza with the community and read the Instructions of St. Theodore the Studite. However, on Saturday and Sunday and on great feast days he would take his meal together with the whole community."

In his free time the Abbot would go with the brothers to their obediences, work side by side with them in the garden, check on the sick, and give counsel to those who came to the monastery for spiritual nourishment. To his monks he would say, "Boys, if you wish to save yourselves, have the fear of God, preserve a pure mind, and do not forget to say the 'Lord Jesus'" [i.e., the Jesus Prayer].

Such was the genuine and lofty spiritual life of the Abbot of the Sihastria Skete. Fr. Ioanichie Moroi was also known to possess the gift of casting out evil spirits. One time, a brother left the monastery without a blessing to go to town to buy something for himself. Along the way seven demons appeared to him in the form of monks, yet horrible and hideous to behold. They charged at him and began to beat him with flaming sticks, violently tormenting him and chasing him through the woods. Still being pursued by the demons, the monk arrived back at the skete, crying out for all to hear, "You won't leave me alone! There are seven after me! You won't leave me alone! There are seven after me!"

The brothers, seizing him, bound him and told the Abbot the situation. He prayed the prayers of absolution for blasphemy and the prayers for casting out evil spirits. Then he told the brothers to unbind him. The brothers, however, said to him, "But what if he runs again?" The Abbot answered, "Do not be afraid! If God has absolved him, bind him no longer!" And so, through the prayers of the Abbot, the brother was made completely whole.

9
Entrance into the Monastery

Upon reaching the gate of Sihastria Skete, the Ilie brothers were met by a stern-looking monk with wild red hair, which gave him the appearance of a ferocious lion. Immediately he began to question Constantine, "Have you come to remain with us?"

Constantine meekly replied, "Yes, your holiness."

The forceful monk, who was the steward of the monastery, informed him that he would tell the Abbot and ordered him to stay outside the gate. The fiery steward quickly returned, holding a stick in his hand, and led Constantine to a

Fr. Cleopa (Novice Constantine) at seventeen years of age.

dead tree trunk. He turned to him and said, "Beat this trunk, beat it!" and without another word he walked away.

All day long Constantine beat the trunk.* Monks and visitors passed by all day but took no notice of him. The lunch bell rang and still no one. Finally, in the late evening, the steward came and, without a word, led him to a room with a bed of board, no blanket, and a straw pillow. Constantine lay his wearied body down to sleep, but before he had dozed off he heard the rhythmic beating of the semantron being sounded for church. It was 11:00 P.M. and the Midnight Office had begun. He was silently led to church and sat in the back. After the services ended and all the monks had departed, the steward led him back to his room.

Very early the next morning, as the birds were meeting the dawn with their morning song, Constantine was roused from bed and led to the front gate and the stump and told only two words, "Beat it!"

The second day proceeded as the first and, again, a third day. Finally, as the sun gave up its light, the formerly austere steward came walking to the front gate. This time, however, there was in his face an observable cheerfulness. "Come, the Elder is calling for you. Leave the stick here."

Constantine was led to Abbot Ioanichie, who asked him, "The stump at the entrance—what did it say to you?"

"It didn't say anything, most pious one."

"Good, let it be so with you."

Fr. Ioanichie then confessed young Constantine and, after receiving his documents, said to him, "You say that you are the brother of Ilie [i.e. Monk Gerasim]? It is not good that you should be together from the beginning. Tomorrow go to the

---

* At this time Basil was separated from Constantine. He was tested in the same manner.

sheepfold to help Anthony Olaru. He is the shepherd in charge of the sheepfold. Listen to him. And Saturday evening come to Confession. Now go."

Waiting outside the Abbot's cell was the steward, "Well, did he ask you for your documents?" he asked, knowing that this would be an indicator of whether he was accepted into the monastery or not.

"Yes, he asked me for my documents," replied the newly accepted novice.

"Good, let's go eat."

Fr. Cleopa would always remember the sacrifice that the steward had secretly made on his behalf. "We ate together because the steward had fasted while my vocation was put to test, and then he led me to another cell, side by side with the brothers."*

10

The Sheepfold

The next morning Constantine was led to the sheepfold in the fertile valley of Sihastria, surrounded by the beautiful and majestic Carpathian Mountains. The breeze of silence gently blew across the hillside above the valley, whispering to the aspiring hearts of young Basil and Constantine a reminder of the presence of the Creator. Day flowed into day as time passed imperceptibly. The brothers rarely left the fold and did not even perform the customary cycle of services. Rather, they sought the altar of God within themselves, continually raising their mind's eye to God through the sacred Prayer of the Heart.

---

* From *Traditsie si Libertate in Spiritualitatea Ortodoxa* by Metropolitan Antonie Plamadeala.

It was here at the sheepfold that the soul of the future spiritual guide of the Romanian people would be formed. Elder Cleopa would later remember his beginnings with nostalgia: "In the years when I was shepherd of the sheep of the skete, together with my brothers, I had great spiritual joy. The sheepfold, the sheep—I lived in quiet and solitude on the mountain, in the midst of nature; it was my monastic and my theological school.

"It was then that I read *Dogmatics* by St. John Damascene and his *Exact Exposition of the Orthodox Faith.* How precious this time was to me! When the weather would warm up, we would put the yearling lambs and the rams in Cherry Meadow, where there was green grass. It was surrounded by bushes, and they would not stray from there. 'Stay put!' I'd say to them, and then I would read *Dogmatics.*

"When I would read something about the Most Holy Trinity, the distinction between angels, man and God, about the qualities of the Most Holy Trinity, or when I would read about Paradise and hell—the dogmas about which St. John Damascene wrote—I would forget to eat that day.

"There was an old hut in which I'd take shelter, and someone from the monastery would bring me food there. When I would return to the hut in the evening, I would ask myself, 'Have I eaten anything today?' Then I'd see the food there and I'd say, 'I haven't eaten!' All day long I was occupied with reading the *Dogmatics* of St. John Damascene. I would put a crocus into my book for a bookmark. When I was with the sheep and cattle, I read St. Macarius of Egypt, St. Macarius of Alexandria, and the *Lives of Saints,* of which I had all twelve volumes. These I brought from Cozancea Skete in my shoulder bag when I first arrived at the monastery. I would read and the day would pass by in what seemed like an hour. The *Lives of Saints* really strengthens one ... very much so.

"So, children, always have a book with you.... In those years I prayed a lot and read the Holy Scriptures and many writings of the Holy Fathers, such as *The Patericon*, *The Ladder* by St. John Climacus, the books of St. Theodore the Studite, St. Isaac the Syrian, St. Ephraim the Syrian, *The Fountain* by St. John Chrysostom, *The Hexaemeron* of St. Basil the Great, and others. I would borrow these books from the libraries of Neamts and Secu Monasteries and carry them with me in my knapsack on the mountain. After I would finish my prayer rule, I'd take out these books of the Holy Fathers and read them next to the sheep until evening. And it seemed as if I saw Saints Anthony, Macarius the Great, John Chrysostom, and the others; how they would speak to me! I would see St. Anthony the Great with a big white beard and a luminous appearance, and he would speak to me in such a way that everything he said would remain imprinted on my mind like when one writes on wax with one's finger. All that I read then I will never forget."

II

Meeting with St. John the Romanian *

At the same time that Br. Constantine was beginning his monastic life at the sheepfold, there labored at the neighboring Neamts Monastery the young brother John Jacob. This young monk worked in the great library of Neamts, amidst the vast

---

* St. John was a monk of Neamts Monastery who went to the Holy Land in 1936 and remained there for the rest of his life. For the last eight years of his life, he labored in the cave of St. Anna, together with one disciple, and reposed on August 5, 1960. Twenty years later his relics were found incorrupt and he was glorified as a saint. His relics were then brought to the Monastery of St. George the Chozebite and are a common site of pilgrimage.

St. John the Romanian (left) as a young monk with two other monks
at Neamts Monastery in the 1930s.

quantity of books and precious manuscripts. Br. Constantine would come to him to borrow books. In 1934 he borrowed *The Spiritual Alphabet* by St. Dimitry of Rostov. In the summer of that year Br. John Jacob came to the sheepfold with the steward of Neamts and asked, "Br. Constantine, have you finished reading the book *The Spiritual Alphabet?*"

"I have a little more to read and after I finish I will bring it to the library," he replied to the future Saint of the Holy Land.

"Good, Br. Constantine. God help you on the path to salvation! At Neamts Monastery there are many holy books. Read them now while you are young, because in old age you will have other cares!" said Br. John Jacob, hinting at the position of leadership that the young Constantine would later assume.

12

First Instructor—Fr. Galacteon

At the sheepfold there was an experienced older monk, Fr. Galacteon, who guided the young Constantine. He was born of poor parents in the village of Pipirig in the Neamts region, and in his youth he was the shepherd of the sheep of the village.

Fr. Galacteon was himself a great faster and would not eat until he had completed his entire prayer rule for the day. When the brothers would call him to eat, the guileless Elder would answer, "Forgive me brothers, I haven't fulfilled my obligation to God. How can I eat when I haven't done my duty?" The Elder would withdraw into the woods to finish his prayers with prostrations, and only then would he take a little food.

On Wednesdays and Fridays the Elder would not eat at all until after the first stars had appeared in the sky. Then he would cross himself, ask forgiveness of everyone, eat a piece of holy bread, and quietly eat in the presence of his brothers. Once a disciple asked him, "Fr. Galacteon, the day is long and your holiness is weak and old. Wouldn't it be better to allow yourself to have the meal a little earlier?"

"Br. Constantine, hear what Fr. Athanasius of Neamts Monastery said to me: 'Once a saint saw how a dead man was being taken to the grave, and in front of and behind the dead man were two beautiful angels. Then the saint asked them, "Who are you?" And the angels answered, "I am called Wednesday." "And I am Friday! We have come here by the order of God to help this soul, who all his life fasted on Wednesday and Friday in honor of the Passion of Christ."' Since the time Fr. Athanasius told me this narrative, I haven't eaten anything on these days, so that the holy angels of Wednesday and Friday will also help me at the hour of death."

If this humble father saw someone passing by the sheepfold, he would immediately say to his disciple, "Br. Constantine, go and call that man to come eat with us, because the sheepfold is like a spring, and if you don't give anything from it, the spring will dry up. But if you give something, God keeps the sheep healthy, and there is no concern for how much is left over, because in giving, the blessing of the Lord is upon us."

His disciples would also say that they never saw Fr. Galacteon eat alone or in secret. If he received some food from the monastery, he would not taste anything until he had come to the sheepfold. He would call everyone to partake equally.

"Why don't you eat alone, Fr. Galacteon?" the brothers would ask him.

"The greatest danger is for a monk to eat in secret!" he would answer. Then, with his heart full of peace, he would add, "Brothers, love and brotherhood surpass great riches and wealth!"

Fr. Galacteon was the poorest monk in the monastery. He had a single set of clothes, a sheepskin coat and a few clean linens. Once his disciple asked him, "Why doesn't your holiness have for himself some good clothes like the other Fathers have?"

The Elder replied, "Br. Constantine, I confessed to a desert-dweller whom I met while walking with the sheep on the mountain. He said to me, 'Fr. Galacteon, have only enough belongings so that you can carry them at one time on your back when you move from one place to another.'"

Another time the Elder met a holy desert-dweller in the woods and asked him, "Tell me, Father, when will the end of the world be?"

"Do you know when the end of the world will come? When there will no longer be a pathway from neighbor to neighbor. That is, when love will be absent among men!" answered the holy ascetic.

In the evenings Fr. Galacteon would have the brothers gather around and read from the *Patericon* and from the Holy Scriptures, for he delighted much in the Word of the Lord.

Once he said to his disciple, "Br. Constantine, please read me more from the Holy Scriptures about the patience of Job!"

While Br. Constantine would read, Fr. Galacteon would weep and say, "Behold, this was a great man, because he did not grumble against God when He took so many sheep, so much cattle, and his children. And I, the sinner, how weak I am in faith! If I become sick or lose any sheep, I can't even eat that day!"

"Why can't you eat when that happens?" asked Br. Constantine.

"How can I be so bold as to eat when I see that God punishes the flock because of my sins?"

In the fall of 1946, after nearly thirty years of obedience, Fr. Galacteon broke his leg. While lying in bed and waiting for his end, he heard that a monk named Nazarius had died. He called for his disciple at the sheepfold, Fr. Cleopa, who was by now the Abbot, and entreated him, "Please, Father Abbot, do not bury Fr. Nazarius without me! Don't spend the money twice. Tomorrow evening at six o'clock, I also will depart from this life!"

On the next day, at the foretold hour, Fr. Galacteon, the good soldier of Christ, gave his spirit into the hands of the Lord. On that day he was sixty-four years old. Such was the end of this son of obedience and Fr. Cleopa's first spiritual father in the monastery.

13
Trials

Like all monks who earnestly seek to purify themselves spiritually, Br. Constantine, as a novice, faced continual trials and tribulations.

At one time Br. Constantine read in a book that monks must, without fail, perform the full cycle of services. Being full of zeal to fulfill every command of the Holy Fathers, Constantine began to diligently perform the services, to such a point that he came to know them by heart. At times, however, the sheep would cause him to leave off his prayers and tend to their needs. Becoming frustrated that he could not fulfill all the services, he went to Abbot Ioanichie to tell him the situation. The Abbot asked him, "With whose blessing did you learn them and who told you to do the Hours? You are to read the Morning Prayers and the Akathist to the Mother of God and, in the evening, the Prayers before Sleep and the Paraclesis to the Mother of God, and throughout the day you are to repeat the Jesus Prayer. The Hours are carried out in church for everyone." Thus Constantine was given a lesson not to trust his own understanding and to receive a blessing for every undertaking, no matter how good it might appear to be.

Another time Constantine was sharing a cell with a certain brother named Nicholas, who liked order and cleanliness. Returning to the cell from his obedience, Br. Constantine took off his shoes and entered the cell without shaking out his clothes. When Br. Nicholas saw this he slapped Br. Constantine for his lack of cleanliness.

Constantine ran off without his shoes to tell his older brothers what had happened. But they reproved him saying, "Br. Constantine, where are the wounds of Christ on your body?"

Later Fr. Cleopa would recall, "Look at how my brothers consoled me! I was without any shelter, and Br. Basil, who was the beekeeper at the time, took me in and let me stay in a room where he kept the bee frames."

Fr. Cleopa would also remember: "When I was young I would come to the stable and rest until midnight. There were four disciples who would stay with Peter Ganea. He had a cell, and the rest of us would sleep below on mats, because there were few cells. There were Simon, Nestor, Paul, and myself.

"When the bell rang Peter would say to us, 'Did you hear the Archangel? Hey you, young men, let's go to prayers!' If we didn't go to prayers then we wouldn't get any food.

"Then Peter would say, 'Costachi,* take your shoes.' It was winter then, but because I had *opinci* shoes** I would run barefoot to the chapel and put my cloth wrappings on the

---

* Costachi: a diminutive for Constantine.
** *Opinci* shoes: peasant shoes made of leather with laces over cloth wrapped around the feet and legs.

stove to dry, since they would be completely wet. I would stand barefoot there and he'd say to the Elder, Ioanichie Moroi, 'Father Abbot, this boy is standing in the corner behind the door and he runs barefoot through the snow. He'll get sick!'

"But the Elder would say, 'Let him be an ascetic!'"

It was discovered that Br. Constantine had a talent for painting icons. For a time he was given a dispensation from his obedience at the sheepfold to learn this sacred art.

"When I was a brother I had the talent for painting. A monk Nilus, of Secu Monastery, taught me how to paint icons. After I had become accustomed to the drawing and painting with watercolors, I began with paints. Sometimes the Abbot would come to my cell, look at how I had painted, and tell me that he liked it. But I had begun to be tempted by money, because I myself would buy the paints and the things I had need of for the painting of holy icons.

"One time the Abbot came to me and tested me, 'What is the price of that icon?'

"'It doesn't have a price, Holy Father' I answered.

"'And that one, Brother Costica, put a high price on it because it is beautiful!' the Elder tested me.

"When I saw that I would have to haggle with men to have money, I became afraid that I would not conquer within myself pride and the love of money. Then one day Fr. Cyriacus, the steward of the skete, came to my cell and said to me, 'Brother Costachi, leave the painting and go to your obedience!' So I left it for good and was sent to graze the sheep.

"Thus I was delivered from two sins: the pride of life and the love of money."

One time Br. Constantine was serving in the Altar and was given the following lesson about attentiveness:

"Once, when Abbot Ioanichie Moroi was serving, after the sanctification of the Gifts, a drop of the Holy Blood jumped out of the Holy Chalice and onto the Holy Anti-mension. This drop began to shine and then to spread beams [of light]. Abbot Ioanichie then called out to me, 'Br. Constantine, come here!'

"When I came he said to me, 'What do you see here on the Holy Antimension?'

"'I see a drop of the Holy Blood shining so strongly that I can hardly look.'

"'Do you see Whom it is we serve? That is why we must stand with great fear and piety in the Holy Altar!'"

Another time Fr. Cleopa recalled a lesson he received on insensitivity:

"In the monastery there was a priest with an ulcer who would serve. Because of his condition, he was not able to tolerate the smoke from the censer.

"Many times this priest told me to be more attentive and to put on less incense; but I, being inattentive, erred con-stantly. The priest, seeing this, did not say anything to me but grieved within himself. One night, after I had come back from Matins and had gone to bed, I had a frightening vision and saw this priest surrounded by rays of light.

"Then I realized that he led a holy life. I ran quickly to him and begged forgiveness. Then I went to the Abbot that night and confessed, telling him my error."

14
Christopher the Hesychast

One time Basil and Constantine were herding the sheep through the trackless forest, when they came upon a desert cell. They slowly knocked and announced themselves, "Father, bless!"

But no one answered. They quietly entered the cell and found different prayer books and a note which read, "Here lives the beast of the earth, D.C." Wishing that they had brought some food for the desert-dweller, they reluctantly returned to the sheepfold.

A few days later a tall, thin monk arrived at the sheepfold.

"Brothers," he said, "I know you from when you came with the sheep to my cell. I saw you from the thicket in the woods. I am the 'beast of the earth,' Hierodeacon Christopher."

"What do you have in that knapsack, with the sign of the Cross on it?" the brothers asked.

"It is the skull of a saint that I found in the forest. Take me to the monastery, to the Father Abbot, so I can reveal this mystery to him."

When they had brought him to Abbot Ioanichie, Hierodeacon Christopher told them the following story:

"This summer, on the day of St. Elias, after serving the Divine Liturgy at Sihla, I was returning to my hut in the forest. On the road I grew weary and slept a little in a clearing. Suddenly an unseen hand turned me around, so that my head was where my feet had been. I thought it was a diabolical deception and crossed myself and went back to sleep. Then the same hand woke me again. At that moment I saw, high up in the fir trees, a very holy monk. He was dressed in a homespun ryassa; his head was uncovered and his white hair hung down his back. His beard was of medium length and his face luminous, and he carried a wooden prayer rope in his hand. He said the following to me in a calm voice: 'Fear not, Fr. Christopher. I am a humble slave of Christ, who long ago, unknown to anyone, lived the ascetic life in this place for many years, and I reposed here. My bones, however, are still unburied. Therefore arise, say the Confession of Faith, and then go a hundred paces to the right, and you will find my bones beside a cliff. You may take only my head for a blessing and carry it with you all your life, wherever you go, for it will be a great help to you. However, do not dare to take my bones, but bury them there under the earth.'

"After the Saint disappeared from before my eyes," continued Hierodeacon Christopher, "I first prayed not to be deceived by the enemy. Then I felt great spiritual joy in my heart. I said the 'I believe' and counted out a hundred paces to the right. Straightway I found, in a hollowed-out cliff, the bones of this great Saint. They were as yellow as wax and fragrant. I crossed myself, made three prostrations, and bent down to fulfill the command. My thoughts, however, tempted me to take all the bones. Therefore I spread the ryassa out on the ground, but—O the wonder!—when I touched the bones they became burning hot in my hand, so that my fingers were burnt. Then, one by one, they disappeared into the earth. Then, asking forgiveness of the Saint for transgressing his command, I took with me only his skull and went to my hut.

"Since that day I carry the Saint's head with me wherever I go, and by his prayers I am delivered from any temptation or danger."

"Fr. Christopher," the Abbot asked him, "do you know the name of this Saint?"

"For a long time I did not know his name. Then I prayed to God with tears to reveal it to me. And one night, when I was celebrating Matins in my hut, this wondrous Saint appeared to me and said, 'Fr. Christopher, do not grieve that you do not know how I am called. My name is Hieroschema-monk Paul. Remember me in your holy prayers.' And immediately he disappeared."

"Yes, he was the spiritual father of St. Theodora of Sihla," said the Abbot. "He lived in Sihastria Skete at the end of the seventeenth century. Then he retired to the desert and reposed there."

Hierodeacon Christopher remained for three days at Sihastria, serving the Liturgy with Abbot Ioanichie. The head of Hieroschema-monk Paul remained on the Holy Altar during that time and exuded a sweet spiritual fragrance throughout the church. Then, after all the fathers had venerated the head of the Saint, Hierodeacon Christopher took his knapsack with the skull in it and departed into the wilderness. No one ever heard of or saw Fr. Christopher again.

15
The Power of the Psalms

In the summer of 1930 Basil and Constantine received a blessing to accompany their brother George in order to help him obtain his release from the military. While they traveled they walked ten to fifteen steps apart from each other, so as to strive continually to say the Prayer of the Heart and the Psalms of David. After making their first stop at the Monastery of St. John the New of Suceava, they arrived at nightfall in a village, without a place to stay. A pious Christian woman, seeing the brothers, asked if they needed anything.

"We are looking for a house to lodge in for the night and we have not found one," they replied.

"We have a house on the outskirts of the village, where no one lives. But I don't know if you will be able to stay in it, because due to the activity of some witches it is haunted by demons," she told them.

"If you will receive us, we will sleep in it."

"Well, brothers, let's go there."

Arriving at the house, the brothers ate something and, being exhausted from their travels, went straight to bed. Before long the evil spirits began making a ruckus in the attic and woke up the brothers. Immediately the brothers jumped up, lit some candles, and prayed for several hours. They continued to hear noises—the shouting and crying out of the demons. Undaunted by the challenge to their prayer from the demonic forces, the brothers persevered in reading the Psalter until things finally quieted down. Toward dawn they heard a few final screams before peace was restored to that possessed house.

In the morning the woman came and asked them how they had slept. Learning of the young monks' victory over the evil spirits, she asked them how to cleanse her house of the spirits. The brothers counseled her to read the Psalter in the evening, at midnight, and in the morning; to have the priest bless the house with holy water, to fast, and to go to Confession.

After their journey they returned through that same village, where they again stayed the night. The Christian woman of the house received them and joyfully announced that from the night that the young monks had first stayed in her house and prayed, it had no longer been haunted. From this the woman understood the power of the Psalms of David.

16
Br. Constantine Is Healed

One spring Br. Constantine suffered from severe hemorrhaging of the lungs. Fr. Galacteon sent him off to collect nettle roots and told him to make a broth of the roots and drink it. Br. Constantine fulfilled the orders of the Elder and was quickly healed.

Years later, after he had become the Abbot of Sihastria, he traveled to the capital of Bucharest on business and spoke to the faithful in four different places all in one day. One pious old lady, who had known Fr. Cleopa since his youth when he had lung problems, was amazed at how powerful and untiring his voice was. Fr. Cleopa also visited a doctor, Athanasius, for a checkup. Dr. Athanasius marveled after seeing the X ray and asked, "What did you do, Father? You have grown a new lung!" and Fr. Cleopa told him how he had drank the nettle broth and with God's help had been cured.

17
Ryassaphore Monk Basil (1905–1931)

From the day Constantine and Basil first arrived at the front gate of Sihastria Skete, the two brothers had labored together at the sheepfold. Br. Basil was known for his meekness and loving disposition. As a reflection of his graceful character, even the sheep, the dogs, and the birds loved him, as well as all the brothers. He at only once a day, after 3:00 P.M. He knew the Psalter, the church services, and many Akathists by heart, and would say them daily as he followed after the sheep with his head uncovered. He would make five hundred prostrations at night and read the *Lives of Saints,* always pondering on the judgments of the Lord.

To this sensitive soul, so beloved of Christ, was given the obedience of caring for the desert-dwellers in the mountains surrounding the sheepfold. At that time there were over forty monks and nuns laboring in asceticism in the region of Sihastria and Sihla Sketes. Whenever Br. Basil would meet one of these strugglers hidden from the world's eyes, he would make a prostration and say, "Bless me, Father, and pray for me a sinner! Do you need me to bring you any food from the sheepfold?"

A desert-dweller in Romania.

If the desert-dweller consented, the next day Basil would bring him cheese, potatoes, vegetables, salt, and flour. While delivering the provisions, he would often ask the Elders for a profitable word.

Once he asked a desert-dweller, "Father, what must I do to be saved?"

"Br. Basil," replied the Elder, "pray constantly, do your obedience with love, and have humility. If you guard these three, you will surely be saved."

18
The Prophecy of St. John the Bishop*

At this time there lived in the neighboring wilderness a certain Bishop John. He had attained such holiness that he was sustained solely by partaking of the Body and Blood of Christ, and this only rarely.

This desert-dweller was a Russian by birth, and in 1915 he was ordained vicar bishop of Kiev. When the Bolshevik Revolution struck, he crossed the border to Romania and eventually ended up in southern Romania at Crasna Skete, where he cared for the sheep in the guise of a novice. When the Abbot sought to tonsure him a monk, he fled northward to the Sihla Mountains and lived there as a desert-dweller.

Br. Basil and Br. Constantine were grazing the sheep on the summit of the Sihla Mountains. Basil was in front of the sheep and was praying, while Constantine was following the herd. Suddenly the desert-dweller appeared, accompanied by a deacon. After blessing them both, Bishop John gave this message through the deacon, who knew the Romanian language: "Br. Basil, prepare to go on ahead, because you have to make a long journey!"

Constantine did not understand these words, but Br. Basil understood that the holy man had made a prophecy and that he must prepare himself for death. Although this mystic was rarely seen by men, he had a close spiritual connection with the future Abbot Cleopa. He would even go to services at Sihastria but remain mysteriously unnoticed by the monks. Many believe that he would secretly converse with Fr. Cleopa,

---

* See his Life in *The Orthodox Word* no. 162 (1992), pp. 43–50, and in the forthcoming *Romanian Patericon*, vol. 2.

Bishop John prophesying the early repose of Br. Basil.

while others maintain that their friendship was purely spiritual and that their mystical bond was forged through holy prayer, in which they were united in Christ.

19
The Marvelous End of Br. Basil

In the spring of 1931, the humble ascetic and older of the two shepherd brothers fell ill and was forced to return to the skete. One morning, as he was leaving church after Liturgy, Br. Basil beheld a frightful vision. Falling on his knees, he cried out, "Most Holy Birthgiver of God, have mercy on me and grant me thy grace to defeat the demons! Do not abandon me!"

And to the fathers who had gathered around him, he said, "Cross yourselves, Fathers! Cross yourselves because, behold, our Lady has come! Behold, the Mother of God is in front of us with the Savior in her arms! Behold her over us!"

"Br Basil, why did you cry out so loudly?" the monks asked him.

"Fathers, when I began to pray in front of the church, all of a sudden a band of very fierce demons with flaming sticks began to beat me and accuse me, 'In vain do you pray, because you aren't saving yourself. You are ours, because you are a sinner!' Then I began to call out with hope to the Mother of God. In that very moment a white cloud descended from heaven, full of light, over the entire church. And in the cloud I saw the Mother of the Lord, with the Babe in her arms, saying to me, 'Do not be afraid, because three days from now you are coming to us!' Then the Savior blessed us all and the cloud was borne aloft to Heaven.... Fathers, the Mother of the Lord has great power and boldness before our Savior Jesus Christ. He listens to her prayers"

Abbot Ioanichie then warned Br. Basil, "Br. Basil, do not let the enemy deceive you. Take heed to yourself and guard your mind, for many are his snares."

The Abbot told the brothers, "If after three days Br. Basil is taken from us, then in truth the Mother of the Lord has appeared to him. And if not, then he has been deceived by the devil."

After three days, the truth was revealed, as Br. Basil gave his soul into the hands of God at that very hour. How many holy desert-dwellers must have been praying for him in that very hour, when the twenty-six-year-old ryassaphore monk finished his earthly course—went on his "journey," as the desert-dwelling mystic had foretold!

20

Monk Gerasim Ilie (1907–1933)

Monk Gerasim was perhaps the most ascetic of the three brothers in the flesh and spirit. He led a life of exalted mystical asceticism. He knew both the Psalter and the cycle of services by heart and repeated them daily. He was known to keep Vigil throughout the night, slapping himself to keep awake, pouring out his tears and begging God's mercy. He spoke little and had a great devotion to the Mother of God.

Fr. Gerasim always carried in his knapsack an icon the Mother of God, which he wrapped in a clean cloth, and the *Lives of Saints*. He would take his sack and depart to tend the cattle in the pasture, or he would go into the woods, hang the icon on the trunk of a beech tree, sing the Akathist to her, and make prostrations. One day he was especially struck with contrition and began to shed many tears before the Mother of the Lord. A forester happened to pass by at that moment and

Br. George Ilie, later Monk Gerasim, when he was in the army.

asked with concern, "What happened to you, Father, that you are crying so?"

"I hit my leg."

"It's all right, Father, it will pass!"

"May God grant that it pass from me!"

In this way Fr. Gerasim concealed the secrets of his heart, in which were hidden great spiritual treasures.

This young soldier of Christ also performed a secret practice of meditating on death and the fearful judgment. To bring the reality of death closer to him, he would visit those who had fatal illnesses and were approaching their end, pray with them, read to them from holy books, and thus bring himself to tears at the nearness of death and console those who were preparing for the other world.

At night he would go to the cemetery to pray and weep at the graves of the fathers who had passed from this earthly vale. In his cell he built a coffin for a bed, and in it he slept a few hours toward morning.

Fr. Cleopa would tell stories of his brother's struggles: "He would sleep three hours, at the most four, after Matins. I went to the Abbot and told him, 'Father Abbot, I can no longer stay with Fr. Gerasim. All the night long he slaps himself and weeps.' Sometimes he would weep for two hours. He would cry so hard that you would think his shirt was jumping off him. And afterwards he'd only struggle even harder.

"'My boy, let him be. That is his work. You do not know his struggle,' the Abbot said."

Such was the violent asceticism of Fr. Gerasim. Suddenly he took ill and the Abbot asked him, "Will you let us take you to the doctor to regain your health?"

But he answered with tears, "Forgive me, Fathers, I have prayed to God to give me trouble and illness so that through them I will be saved. Therefore, how can I refuse this illness?

Leave me in the hands of God, because this illness is toward my salvation."

Like his older brother Basil, Fr. Gerasim would not live to see his thirtieth year in this world. Both died at twenty-six. In a short time they had become ripe for God, burning in spirit and longing for Paradise, a foretaste of which they had already experienced in their short lives.

In his sickness Fr. Gerasim could not attend the daily cycle of church services, but he would never miss the Liturgy. His brothers would bring him a blanket and lay him down in the narthex.

Some would say to him, "Fr. Gerasim, why don't you stay in your cell until you are well?"

"Fathers, forgive me, a sinner. I came to listen to the Holy Liturgy. Perhaps this is the end of my life. There is no service that we have more need of for our salvation than the Holy Liturgy."

One day an old monk died. Fr. Gerasim then said to all with tears, "Know, Fathers, that it is my turn to depart from this life, after Br. Basil."

Indeed, on September 14, 1933, on the Feast of the Exaltation of the Holy Cross, the cross-bearing monk Gerasim committed his soul into the hands of God. He was found lying in the coffin he had made with his own hands. Under the head of the bed was found a letter addressed to his younger brother Constantine:

"My beloved brother Constantine, know that God will preserve you longer in this life. Therefore, please do not forget me the sinner in your holy prayers, since with many tears I have prayed for you and all the brothers, that the Lord will guide you on the path of salvation."

21

Heavenly Vision of Br. Constantine

During the forty days following the death of his brother Gerasim, Constantine read the Psalter, fasted, and prayed for his salvation. One day he dozed off for a short while. In his dream he saw that his brother's grave in the old cemetery of the church was open and that the lid of the coffin was set aside; from the Holy Altar a spring of clear water began to flow like crystal over the tomb, and the image of his brother became white like snow. Then Fr. Gerasim awoke as if from sleep and said, "Br. Constantine, the prayers of the Church saved me...."

In that same year, deeply saddened at the loss of the two who were so close to him in spirit, Constantine prayed that God would reveal their fate to him. One evening he fell asleep in his cell and he did not wake up until morning, sleeping through the church services.

Upon waking, he was calm and reconciled in spirit. Then he went to the Abbot and told him of the vision he had seen that night. He said that he had met with his brothers, together with his sisters who had also departed this life at an early age. They were in a wonderful garden full of flowers and good fragrance, with fruit trees laden with fruits, while heavenly birds were singing praises to God. The entire night he spent together with his brothers, walking with them and singing with great spiritual joy in the garden of Paradise.

Finally his brothers said good-bye to him and promised to pray for him so that one day they would all be together. They exhorted him to be obedient and to pray unceasingly, because after a time he would be a guide of souls. Then they de-

The graves of Ryassaphore monk Basil and Monk Gerasim in the Sihastria Cemetery.

parted jumping for joy, and Constantine awoke from his deep sleep. It was already five in the morning.

22
Miracle of St. John the New

After seeing his two closest companions in life buried, and having received a confirmation as to their place in heaven, Constantine desired to visit the last of his nine siblings still alive on earth. His sister Catherine was a nun at Old Agapia Monastery.

Following a trail deep into the woods, Constantine suddenly found himself surrounded by wild boars. Fearing his own demise, he began to sing in a loud voice the kontakion of St. John the New of Suceava: "Defender and helper of Christians...."

Nun Catherine Ilie, sister of Elder Cleopa.

In that moment he no longer saw anything around him. Without lingering, he climbed to the peak of the hill and collapsed from exhaustion. After coming to himself, he continued on his journey and only with great difficulty did he reach his sister at Old Agapia.

23

Departure to the Army

Br. Constantine was called into the service of the army in 1935. He had now been a novice in the monastery for six years. He took leave of the brothers at the sheepfold and came down to the skete, where he confessed to the Abbot, received Holy Communion, and said his final prayers before departing for his native village where he was to report for duty.

In the army Constantine continued to live as a monk, abiding in prayer and fasting. He was granted his special request to abstain from eating meat, as he was preparing himself to be a monk. Through his wholehearted devotion to the monastic ideal, Constantine had already achieved a high level of purity.

Often he wore his monastic garb while serving the sick in the infirmary. He maintained his prayer rule and was honest with everyone. Because of his upright dealings with all, he was well respected despite being so young. He led the soldiers in morning and evening prayers in the regiment chapel, and on feast days he led all to services in the church. As Romania was still a Christian nation at this point, many were thankful for his presence and for his life devoted to Christ.

For this reason the military superiors often asked him to talk with certain of the soldiers. Even officers would gather around to listen to his discourse and thereby receive benefit from his words. In special cases, when a soldier would be in urgent need of a priest, Constantine would bring him to the chaplain for Confession and Communion. Others would ask the young monk for spiritual counsel and some about the monastic life.

At the end of his military service it was proposed to him to remain in the army, "Stay here, for with your memory you will attain the rank of General," one officer exhorted him.

But Constantine refused, saying, "I am a soldier in the army of Christ, the King of Kings."

24
The Bond between Schema-monk Paisius and Br. Constantine

The lifelong friendship between Fr. Paisius Olaru and the future Abbot Cleopa was not only a personal bond, but one that would extend its arms to embrace the whole nation of Romania. These two would prove to be spiritual heroes in a time when the country's faith was being persecuted by the communist regime.

In 1936 the young Corporal Constantine Ilie was freed from his military service, but he had to remain in the vicinity of his regiment until his official release. It was during this time that he chose to visit the monk who had nurtured him spiritually as a boy. Overjoyed to see his young zealot, Fr. Paisius asked him, "Tell me, Br. Constantine, if you are free from the army, why don't you come here to me?"

"Holy Father Paisius, I don't want to lie. I am spiritually bound to Sihastria Skete, where I first went and where my brothers fell asleep in the Lord. Here at Cozancea it is too close to my village, and I want to be more of a stranger and unknown by my relatives. After my release I must return to Sihastria."

Hearing this, Fr. Paisius wept and said, "I had hoped that I would have a disciple from your family, but if you do not have the mind to come here after the army, before long I also will go to Sihastria."

Fr. Paisius then accompanied the young soldier-monk to a place where the fields and hills of Constantine's native village could be seen. With tears in his eyes he said, "Come, let us make a vow, but first let us make three prostrations!"

After prayerfully prostrating their bodies to the earth before God's all-seeing eye, the older monk continued, "O Most Holy Trinity, our God, through the prayers of the Most Pure Birthgiver of God and all the saints, vouchsafe that if Br. Constantine dies before me, I will be at his head, and if I die first, he will be at my head. Amen."

With these heartfelt words the two parted in tears. And, indeed, this entreaty of Fr. Paisius' would come to pass, though exactly how would not be revealed until the end of Elder Paisius' life.

25

Tonsure into Monasticism

With a hopeful heart Br. Constantine returned to the monastery of his repentance and the place where he felt called to serve God. Awaiting his return at the sheepfold was his first spiritual father, the humble monk Galacteon, together with Fr. Anthony. Together the three shepherds continued their quiet life of prayer, silence, and caring for God's creatures in the bosom of nature.

By 1937 Br. Constantine had completed six years of discipleship and fulfilled his military duty. He was now able to

A sheepfold in a Romanian monastery today.

make his voluntary offering, wholly devoting his life to Christ
in poverty, chastity, and obedience. As is the custom, he chose
as a sponsor an elder monk who would guide him in the monastic life. Constantine's choice was the venerable Elder, full of
love and humility, Schema-monk Proclus Popa. At first Fr.
Proclus refused, saying, "Br. Costachi, I am so very old. I am
seventy-seven years old and am no longer able. Please look for
someone else to be your sponsor."

"Fr. Proclus, if your holiness will not take me under your
mantle, I won't be tonsured so soon," responded the young ryassaphore monk.

Hearing these words, the Elder rejoiced greatly, saying,
"All right, Br. Constantine, prepare yourself, because tonight
I'll take you under my mantle."

And so the whole brotherhood gathered in the church to
pray that God would strengthen the young aspirant to carry

his cross until the end. As Constantine was brought before the the ambo, just moments before he would be tonsured, one monk named Nicholas spoke out, "Father Abbot, give him the name Cleopa, because we don't have anyone with that name."

"Well said, Fr. Nicholas," said the Abbot from the ambo, and proceeded, "Our brother, Monk Cleopa, is tonsured by the hairs of his head in the name of the Father, of the Son, and of the Holy Spirit!" While the Abbot tonsured him the choir of brethren loudly proclaimed, "Amen, Amen, Amen!" Immediately the Abbot with a loud and triumphant voice exclaimed, "Let us pray to the Lord!" and the brothers all sang out, "Lord have mercy."

As is the custom, the tonsured monk and his sponsor then venerated the icon of the Mother of God and Monk Cleopa was ushered to the cliros. Such was the beginning for one of the greatest monks of Romania in the twentieth century.

26
The Fire of 1941

On May 30, 1941, as the Feast of the Ascension was drawing near and thousands of pilgrims were on their way to worship at Neamts Monastery, the fathers of Sihastria were receiving many of the pilgrims on their way to Neamts. This year there was a terrible drought and a warm dry wind was blowing. All of a sudden one of the wooden cells caught fire and within half an hour the entire enclosure was in flames. All the cells, the roof of the stone church and the wooden chapel dedicated to Sts. Joachim and Anna burned down. It seemed that all was lost.

In the midst of the flames, some courageous souls entered the wooden chapel and removed the Holy Bible, the

Holy Gifts, holy icons, and holy vessels. They could not, however, find where the holy relics were kept. While all were saddened at the loss of the relics, suddenly the white box wrapped with a red ribbon which held the relics was seen miraculously exiting the chapel through the air and then falling into the middle of the courtyard! Seeing the miracle, the fathers picked up the box of relics, kissed them, and praised God with thanksgiving.

Abbot Ioanichie Moroi, seeing all the fruit of his labor over the past thirty years destroyed in less than an hour, fell to the ground with tears in his eyes, made three prostrations toward the church that now stood without a roof, and repeated the words of the righteous Job, *"The Lord gave, and the Lord hath taken away; blessed be the name of the Lord* (Job 1:21). Amen."

In this great misfortune the Abbot did not shrink in despondency but rather, enlarged by faith, rose up and exhorted the brethren, "Fathers, let us not be discouraged because the monastery has burned. It burned because of our sins and in order to renew the foundations! Endure all temptations with strength and do not abandon this place sanctified by prayer and the tears of our forebears. Only keep with diligence the tradition of this skete. Whoever does not keep the tradition of this place, the place will itself cast him out! Keep the monastic rule and do not leave uncompleted, even for a day, the Divine Liturgy and the cycle of services.

"If you do this and lead a pure life and have love among yourselves, know that the Mother of the Lord will raise up out of the ashes this holy dwelling and you will have peace and salvation in this place. But if you do not preserve in holiness the Rule, fasting, and your monastic duties, know that this place will be laid waste. For God prefers much more a deserted and clean place to a place with many monks and disunity!"

27
How Monk Cleopa Was Chosen Abbot

The year was 1941, the skete had just burned down, and Abbot Ioanichie Moroi was eighty-two years old. After a lifetime of asceticism, and having been beaten by outlaws, Fr. Ioanichie now barely had enough strength to confess the monks and give spiritual counsel. He no longer served the Liturgy. Only his close disciple, Hieroschema-monk Joel (Gheorgiu), was serving. Due to the lack of cells caused by the fire, many of the monks had gone to Neamts and Secu monasteries.

In the midst of this apparent decline, Fr. Ioanichie received a confirmation that the situation was only temporary. While he was sick and troubled about the future of the monastery, a modestly attired woman entered his cell and said to him, "Do not be sad, Fr. Ioanichie. From now on we will take care of this holy dwelling." It was the Most Holy Birthgiver of God, the Patroness of the skete. Indeed, from the following year the protection of the Lord's Mother was espcecially felt over Sihastria.

Feeling his strength waning, the Abbot called together all the fathers and brothers of the monastery for a common council and addressed them: "It is time that I leave this place in the hands of another, Fathers and Brothers. Bless and forgive me a sinner, since I long for rest. Choose another abbot. From now on I choose to be one of those who obey, to weep for the sins which I have acquired during the time it was arranged from Above that I be your counselor. As you holy ones know, it is not easy work to bear the care of many souls. You make mistakes, you get angry like any man, you grieve the brothers, and then you anger God. But the time of error must be redeemed with a time of repentance. And I am weak, and who knows the days of a man? Perhaps tomorrow God will call me and find me unprepared!"

Then the monks said, "Never mind, because we will pray for you. God is compassionate. Stay on. Who could take your place? Your holiness received us all from the world and taught us the road to salvation and the sweetness of meditation on God. Have pity on our souls until the end."

Among the fathers were many with white hair, but all felt as children near their spiritual father. Despite their many entreaties, the Abbot remained resolute in his intention.

"And whom do we choose in your place, Father?" asked a monk named Nathaniel.

"Cleopa," responded the Elder simply, looking at them with a gesture of defiance.

"Which Cleopa?" several asked, jumping as if he had put red-hot coals under their feet.

A few beards had finally started to tremble. Fr. Nathaniel began to bite the ends of his mustache, pulling the hairs one by one with his tongue and putting them between tight lips: crunch, crunch, crunch.... Fr. Nathaniel had coarse hair and his front teeth were whole.

"Cleopa of Foot-of-the-Cross,"* explained the Elder.

"The simpleton of the sheep?"

Upon the faces of several monks appeared smiles. From the back of the assembly Fr. Chesarie, a vigorous old monk with a long red beard speckled with white hairs, translated his knowing smile into words, "The Elder has deteriorated! Old age—what do you expect? Indeed, the time has come for him to rest in his cell."

Eleven years had gone by since the young Constantine had passed through his trial at the front gate and been accepted

---

* The name of the spot where Fr. Cleopa tended the sheep.

into the monastery. In that time he had only left the sheepfold for one year, for his service in the army, and, on occasion, to confess to the Elder in the skete.

The fathers continued to plead with the Elder to recant his choice of successor. They set before him their reasonable concerns and opinions: "Cleopa does not know how to read; Cleopa does not know how to speak with people; he will not be able manage the repair work. Cleopa does not have spiritual experience because he has only stayed in the sheepfold."

Finally they concluded, "We deserve an abbot like Cleopa; it will be the end of the monastery!"

"I say it shall be Cleopa," persisted the Elder. "But you holy ones can choose another. I have only given my opinion, since you asked me. Now I am no longer abbot; I no longer command. I know you are thinking of my disciple Joel, but it will not be Joel now. Joel will be abbot after Cleopa leaves."

This was the bell of prophecy, but no one rose to apprehend the significance of the righteous Elder's words. They were convinced that the Elder had lost his mental balance.

The monks then withdrew among themselves to make a resolution. Fr. Bessarion then proposed an idea: "Fathers, it is not good that we grieve the Elder. He was our father our whole lives. Let us allow him to die in peace. Let us choose Cleopa, the way he wants us to, and we can take care of the monastery. We have a council, do we not? It shall be Cleopa for appearance' sake."

The monks returned and told the Elder that they had chosen Cleopa. The Elder smiled knowingly and was satisfied.

The next day after the Liturgy, in full regalia, the brotherhood of monks made a procession to the sheepfold to greet the new Abbot. Seeing the long procession of monks, Fr. Cleopa shouted to his fellow shepherd, Fr. Anthony, "The community is coming over the hill!"

"They are saying prayers for rain," replied Fr. Anthony, rushing off to put things in order in the sheepfold.

The community drew near silently, solemnly, as if for a funeral. They looked at Cleopa strangely as he stood in front of them clad in dirty and tattered rags.

Fr. Bessarion was the first to step forward. At first he made a bow and then changed his mind and made a full prostration before the simple shepherd-monk, who stared at him in bewilderment.

"Fr. Cleopa, the Elder has retired from his position as abbot and the community has elected your holiness as the new abbot."

At that moment, the entire assembly of monks at once made a full prostration in the grass before their newly chosen abbot. But at the same time, Fr. Cleopa fell to the ground and beckoned the brothers, "I will not rise from the earth until you change the decision. I am not worthy to be abbot."

Fr. Bessarion then began to speak directly and with harshness in his voice, "We know. We all know, Father. But it is an obedience of the Elder. He wants you. We have decided to listen, in order not to grieve him. Who knows how many more days he has, and it is a sin to upset him just now. Accept out of obedience. We will take care of the monastery. Don't worry about that. Let us make the Elder happy."

Hearing the word of command, Fr. Cleopa raised himself up and said with gravity, "If it is from obedience before the Elder, I accept. But Fathers, do not leave me without help."

Fr. Cleopa then asked for time to pray, and he went to speak with Fr. Paisius Olaru. When he came back to the monastery, the monks led him to wash and brought him fresh linen, a thick sheepskin coat, a new robe from the storehouse, and boots in which he could hardly walk. Then they led him into the church for the traditional ceremony of installation.

The Elder also came to church for the event. The secretary read the decision of election without enthusiasm, and without a word the Elder handed Fr. Cleopa the abbot's staff.

Everyone began to stir and prepare to leave the church, when the newly chosen raised his hand to gather the brotherhood's attention.

"Our Abbot knows how to speak!" said one mockingly.

Fr. Cleopa then proceeded to prove that indeed he did know how to speak, and for two hours he gave a discourse on the path to salvation based on the teachings of the Holy Fathers. He cited from memory long passages from St. Isaac the Syrian, St. John Damascene, St. John of the Ladder, and St. Maximos the Confessor, as well as from Paisian manuscripts and contemporary theological works. In addition he proposed a plan of reconstruction for all the buildings lost in the fire and explained precisely how he would continue the tradition of the Elder. Struck with amazement, all the fathers realized that their new Abbot was a true disciple of the great Elder Ioanichie Moroi.

Humbled and full of respect toward their new spiritual leader, and led by the Elder, all the monks came to receive the blessing of Abbot Cleopa.*

28
Rebuilding the Skete

In the fall of 1942 new living quarters, consisting of twenty cells, began to be constructed under the direction of Abbot Cleopa. Lumber was donated generously from Neamts Monastery, and the faithful came to donate their time and construction experience.

* Most of this chapter has been taken from *Traditsie si Libertate in Spiritualitatea Ortodoxa* by Metropolitan Antonie Plamadeala, with slight changes based on the account of Fr. Ioanichie Balan.

At this time World War II was in progress. The proximity of the Soviet Army delayed construction for a period, but after the front passed west of the Carpathian Mountains, building resumed. The young Abbot Cleopa soon proved himself a responsible steward and a spiritual leader who led by his own example. He was also shown to be gifted at speaking, through which he would nourish the souls not only of his monks and pilgrims but also of dispersed refugees who had escaped to the peaceful grounds of Sihastria.

29
The Last Days of Abbot Ioanichie Moroi

After thirty-three years of severe asceticism, Abbot Ioanichie Moroi fell ill. In his illness he was thankful that he had, in Fr. Cleopa, a son who would continue to lead the skete in the same spirit as he had done. During the last two years of his life the Elder spent his time enclosed in his cell, praying and receiving brothers who came to him for spiritual direction.

In August of 1944 his son according to the flesh, Monk Nicander, was shot by Soviet soldiers near the war front. A month later, feeling his end drawing near, the Elder called all the monks to his bedside and gave his final counsel. He exhorted them to pray without ceasing, to be obedient and loving, to love the Holy Church, and to lead a chaste life in Christ. Then, as he begged forgiveness of all and greeted each one with the kiss of peace, he announced three times, "On Tuesday I will go to the Father!" prophesying his death.

On the day foretold, September 3, 1944, the great Abbot and Elder Ioanichie Moroi committed his soul into the hands of God. With many tears the brothers buried their spiritual father in the new cemetery, thus marking the end of an era and the beginning of a new one under the guidance of Fr. Cleopa. Several years later Schema-nun Augustina of Agapia Convent, who had been his wife and the mother of his children, reposed and was buried in the monastery cemetery at Old Agapia Convent. Thus, the two that had separated themselves for sake of the Kingdom of God were joined together again in the world where love never dies.

30
Ordination

With the passing of Elder Ioanichie to the other world, both the practical and spiritual aspects of directing the monastic brotherhood fell upon the shoulders of Fr. Cleopa. Out of humility, and fearing the great responsibility before God, Fr. Cleopa fled from the idea of being ordained a priest. But as it is impossible to hide from God, so too is it impossible for His servants to flee from His omnipotent will. Behold how Providence arranges all for the good of mankind!

In October of 1944 Monk Cleopa traveled with some of the brothers to a skete in Racova to gather grapes from the vineyard. Along the way a pious woman greeted them, carrying in her hands a set of priestly vestments, a Liturgy book, and a staff. "These vestments and holy objects," she said to them, "were left in my house by a military chaplain who stayed with us during the war. Departing further on with the front, he left them in our house, and I don't know what to do with them."

"Sister, take them to a church or a monastery that has need of them, because it is not good to keep these holy objects in your house," replied Fr. Cleopa.

"Please, Father, take the vestments, the book, and the staff! I thank God that I met you so that I could give them to you!"

Taking the holy things, Fr. Cleopa put them in the cart

Young Abbot Cleopa.

and thought to himself, "I wonder why this woman gave these vestments, the staff, and the liturgical book just to me. Perhaps it is a sign that God wants me to be ordained a priest and to guide the brethren of Sihastria Skete with this staff?"

Upon returning from the vineyard, Fr. Cleopa revealed to his confessor what had happened along the road. Seeing clearly the Providence of God, the confessor told him, "Be obedient, Fr. Cleopa, because all of us vowed this at our tonsure and without it we cannot be saved. Who then will lead the community of the skete if everyone runs from responsibility? Because the Holy Fathers say, 'Obedience is life and disobedience is death.'"

Two months later, on December 27, 1944—the day the Church commemorates the Protomartyr Stephen—Monk Cleopa was ordained a hierodeacon. On January 23, 1945, the day of the holy Hieromartyr Clement, Bishop of Ancyra, he was ordained a hieromonk by Bishop Galacteon Cordun, who was at that time the Abbot of Neamts Monastery. Shortly thereafter Fr. Cleopa was officially installed as the Abbot of Sihastria Skete.*

31
Sihastria Skete (1945–1946)

In 1945 the newly built trapeza, which seated over one hundred people, was blessed. During the same year, ten cells and the monastery kitchen were also completed. The following year, ten more cells were finished. Despite the monks' utter poverty, the monastery was being rebuilt through the assistance of their brothers at Neamts and the voluntary labor of the Romanian people.

---

* That is, installed as Abbot by the Bishop, who thus officially confirmed the choice made by the brotherhood of Sihastria. Before this, Fr. Cleopa was Abbot *locum tenens*.

As with all good undertakings for God's sake, Abbot Cleopa and his monks faced much difficulty. Fr. Cleopa remembers the early days as the new Abbot: "When they named me Abbot, it was very difficult. The skete didn't have any necessities. The patronal feast came and we didn't have anything prepared. The cells had burned and the bells had melted and the big church's roof had also been consumed by flames. Then I went to Neamts Monastery to borrow some money. But they did not give it to me because they didn't have any capital funds.

"Then I went to Fr. Joachim Spataru, the man of God. With him was a good Christian from Bucharest, Constantine Valsan, the director general of the telephone company. This man, hearing that we didn't have anything for the patronal feast day, gave me 800,000 lei, which was a lot of money at that time. When I returned to Sihastria, our spiritual father, Fr. Joel, was waiting for me. He had been praying to God that we would receive some help. Hearing of the donation we had received, he was amazed and thanked God."

In the spring of 1946, because of the war, the faithful from a parish in Suceava were evacuated to an area in the wilderness near Sihastria. As an offering to God and out of thanksgiving for being delivered from the danger of the battle front, they built a new winter church dedicated to Sts. Joachim and Anna to replace the one that had burned down in the fire.

In those two years God arranged for many monastic aspirants, both young and old, to come to Sihastria. Some initially came to the monastery to escape the hunger and poverty which threatened the country, while others were drawn by the growing reputation of Fr. Cleopa. It was also during this time that the communists began to take over Romania and to persecute and imprison the spiritual leaders of the Orthodox

Church. Many monasteries were deprived of their spiritual fathers and, as a result, more monks gathered around Abbot Cleopa. Still in his mid-thirties, Fr. Cleopa began his ministry as a leader in reviving monastic life, and as a preacher of the word of God to the faithful who gathered each day to hear him speak.

32
Sihastria Raised to the Rank of Monastery

As Fr. Cleopa's reputation became known throughout the country, the Romanian Patriarchate took notice of the flourishing state of Sihastria Skete. In June of 1947 Sihastria Skete was officially raised to the rank of Monastery; and on September 19 Fr. Cleopa was raised to the rank of Archimandrite by Bishop Valerian Moglan, who addressed him with these words: "Fr. Cleopa, receive this staff. Whoever obeys you, obeys God! Whoever doesn't obey, you could hit with all the sticks in the forest and he still would not become a true man."

33
Fr. Cleopa Tonsures His Mother
into Monasticism

By 1947 Anna Ilie had lost her husband and all ten of her children, except for Fr. Cleopa. Her only consolations in the village were the church and the cemetery. On every feast day she would go to church, and after the service she would walk alone to the cemetery, where she would weep at the graves of her children.

Although her only child remaining on the earth was Fr. Cleopa, she never saw him, as he had given his life wholly to serving God and neighbor. Fr. Cleopa recalled his father's death, which occurred on February 23, 1943: "When Father died Mother sent me telegram after telegram, calling me to the funeral. Later, when we met, Mother asked me, 'Why didn't you come to Father's funeral?'

"'Since I came to the monastery, I no longer have father or mother,' I answered.

"'How so? Am I not your mother?' the old one asked through her tears.

"'Come to the monastery, and then you will be my mother!'"

In late November of 1946 Fr. Cleopa brought his mother from her native village to Sihastria in order to tonsure her. Here she prayed day and night and rejoiced at seeing all the young brothers who were coming to follow Christ in the monastic life together with her son. She, in her motherly way, considered all as her own children and was loved by all.

On September 21, 1947, Anna Ilie was tonsured with the name Agafia. The next spring Fr. Cleopa brought her to the Old Agapia Convent and presented her to the Eldress, Mother Olympiada. For the next twenty years the devout and pious Nun Agafia labored in the ascetic life at Old Agapia with three disciples: Nuns Michaela, Justina, and Julia.

Despite her old age, every day Mother Agafia would carry wood to the kitchen. Sometimes her disciple would say to her, "Mother Agafia, why do you carry wood on your back to the kitchen?" She would answer, "And am I to eat food in vain?"

Mother Agafia was merciful to the poor. When any impoverished person would come to the convent and she had nothing to give him, she would take something from one of her disciples and give it away. "I took a little something from you because I didn't have anything," she would tell her disciple.

Nun Agafia, the mother of Fr. Cleopa.

"That's fine that you took something." Of course they wanted her to keep it for herself but she would always give it away. Even before she was a nun, when she had a family to support, she would never hesitate to give away whatever she could. Her husband, Alexander, would become frustrated with her and scold her, "My woman, in vain did I bring anything home in the cart, because you give everything away!"

From time to time Mother Agafia would travel to Sihastria to see her son and weep at the graves of her ascetic sons who had died young, Basil and Gerasim.

34
A Miracle of the Mother of God

In the summer of 1947 Fr. Cleopa traveled to Bucharest to obtain church vessels for the new chapel. When he arrived in the capital, the fathers from the Patriarchate invited him to a spiritual gathering of the Burning Bush Movement* in the home of the university professor Alexander Mironescu.

Among the numerous priests, professors, and faithful were Archimandrite Benedict Ghius,** Fr. Dositheus Morariu,***

---

* The Burning Bush Movement was formed to teach hesychastic spirituality to the intellectual youth.
** Archimandrite Benedict Ghius (1904–1990) was a guide to the youth in Bucharest while serving as confessor at the Patriarchal Cathedral and laboring in the Burning Bush Movement. He taught in the seminary of Neamts from 1949 to 1954. He was arrested by the communists in 1954 and imprisoned for four years. He served again in the Patriarchal Cathedral from 1958 to 1978. He retired to Cernica Monastery, where he reposed in 1990. Fr. George Calciu saw Fr. Benedict bathed in Uncreated Light while in the altar at Cernica Monastery. See *The Orthodox Word* no. 197 (1997), pp. 295–96.
*** Fr. Dositheus Morariu was a hieromonk who wrote his seminary thesis on St. Seraphim of Sarov, which had an impact throughout Romania.

Gerontius Gheniu, Fr. Dumitru Staniloae* and many other intellectuals. The people would pose questions of a spiritual nature and the fathers would answer. Fr. Cleopa arrived and was received into their midst. The conversation halted. Each one came to receive the young Abbot's blessing, and the assembly waited for him to give a profitable word. Fr. Cleopa began a discourse based on the writings of the Holy Fathers, about the importance of honoring the Most Holy Mother of God.

On the wall directly behind Fr. Cleopa there was hanging an icon of the Mother of God with the Christ Child and the holy Prophet David. As he spoke with grace-filled words, the icon began to shake and produce the sound of a harp. Sensing that this was an otherworldly visitation, the faithful present were filled with tender feeling. Some began to weep, others made the sign of the Cross, others venerated the icon, and some simply began to pray. Archimandrite Benedict was especially moved and began to repeat with contrition, "Mother of the Lord ... Mother of the Lord ... a miracle ... a miracle!"

After a few minutes the icon stopped moving and the pendulum of the grandfather clock, which had stopped, began to swing normally again. The gathered assembly then joined in prayer to the Mother of God, to have mercy on the country and the Romanian people. This miraculous incident greatly strengthened the faith of all present and gave them spiritual consolation. The evening ended with the singing of "It Is Truly Meet" to the Mother of God.

Most of the witnesses of this miracle considered the event as a sign of confirmation to strengthen Orthodox Christians before a time of persecution, which in fact assailed the Romanian nation within the following year.

---

* Fr. Dumitru Staniloae (†1993) was Romania's greatest theologian. His crowning achievement is his Romanian edition of the *Philokalia* in twelve volumes, with commentary.

The icon of the Mother of God before which Fr. Daniel Tudor composed
the Akathist to the Burning Bush. Located at Rarau Skete.

35
Joys and Sorrows

Amidst the successful renewal of Sihastria Monastery there were also manifest many tribulations, especially for Fr. Cleopa. In the region of the monastery there was an infamous band of outlaws known as the "Balta," which had its gang headquarters in the neighboring wilderness. Abbot Ioanichie Moroi had been beaten by them three times in his life.

Toward the end of 1947, soon after the blessing of the new chapel dedicated to Sts. Joachim and Anna, the entire monastery enclosure was encircled by the Balta outlaws. The faithful were held at gunpoint in the church while the thieves raided the monastery storehouse.

Fr. Cleopa remembered this incident: "One night, when I was abbot and was standing in church during the Vigil, Balta and his gang came, took me out of the service and asked me for wine, food, and money. Being that we didn't have anything, they took me and led me into the woods, where they tied me to a tree with the intent to shoot me. Then one of them suggested to the oldest one, 'Don't you remember how he'd give us food when he was at the sheepfold? And now you want to shoot him?' They started to argue among themselves and went into the woods. When they returned they untied me and allowed me to return to the monastery."

The next day Fr. Cleopa went to Bishop Valerian of Neamts and asked him for advice. "Your Holiness, what should we do for the monastery to be delivered from the outlaws who have been robbing us and causing unrest for the past six years?"

"Fr. Cleopa, you know what you must do? Have a Vigil to

the Protection of the Mother of God every Tuesday evening and read the Psalter day and night in church, each one reading for two hours, from the abbot down to the last brother. If you do this, the Mother of God will drive away these outlaws and will bless you with all that you need, and the monastery will be guarded from all dangers."

Hearing these words, Abbot Cleopa ordered that a Vigil to the Protection of the Mother of God be served on the following Tuesday and that the Psalter be read continuously between services. And, indeed, the evildoers were caught and punished according to the law.

This practice is continued to the present day in Sihastria Monastery, which since that time has spiritually flourished through the intercessions of the Most Pure Theotokos.

36
The Lost Sheep

While Fr. Cleopa was abbot at Sihastria, it so happened that the shepherds lost the sheep. For some time they searched but did not find them, and the brothers were afraid to tell the Abbot. Finally they had no choice and came to Fr. Cleopa. He listened to them and then led them to church, where they all knelt down before the icon of the Mother of God and began to pray. After they had prayed, Fr. Cleopa said to them, "Come, let us go together toward Sihla and Falcon's Cliff!"

Along the way they continually made short stops to pray for guidance. At last, with God's help, they arrived at a small meadow where they found the sheep quietly resting. Then Abbot Cleopa addressed the brothers: "What great joy we have because we have found the sheep, and thousands of times greater because God has guided us. Behold what I say unto

Abbot Cleopa with a sheep dog and sheep.

you: Do not begin anything that you do in your life without prayer before God and the Mother of God."

Returning with the sheep toward the valley, they made just as many short stops to pray in thanksgiving as they had made on their journey to find the sheep.

37
How Fr. Cleopa Delivered a Woman from Death

During the Nativity Fast of 1947 Fr. Cleopa was confessing many people until past midnight and was exhausted. Just when he was going to rest, a woman who was crying approached him: "Father, I will be here only six hours—I came to confess because I have heavy sins on my soul!"

"Woman, I am tired. Please come in the morning."

"Father, if you will not receive me for Confession, I will go and kill myself. Look, I have a rope with me! I have committed heavy sins and I have aborted many children. Receive me, because I can no longer endure!"

Fr. Cleopa then confessed her, giving her the strength to go on. He gave her a penance and absolved her from the grave sins which had weighed on her conscience and bound her spirit like iron shackles. The next day she was given to drink holy water from the Great Blessing of Waters on Theophany. She returned to her home at peace and spiritually renewed. And in many other cases Fr. Cleopa gave hope to the hopeless, consoled the sorrowing, and helped to revive souls perishing from the weight of life and their sins.

38
Elder Paisius Olaru Enters Sihastria

Desiring to unite himself and his monks to his first spiritual father and the monk closest to him in spirit, Fr. Cleopa arranged for Elder Paisius Olaru to come to stay permanently at Sihastria. The arrival of Fr. Paisius was also mystically connected with the vow they had made together when the young Constantine was returning to the monastery from the army.

Elder Paisius came to Sihastria as a recently ordained priest-monk. Due to his experience in the monastic life, he was immediately a source of consolation for the brothers and a pillar of support to Abbot Cleopa in the governing of the monastic life at Sihastria. He became the Confessor not only of the monks but also of hundreds of lay people who would flock to Sihastria to drink from the living waters of grace. On the average he would confess fifty to a hundred monks and lay people a day. Thus it was only through the power of God that he had the strength to carry the weight of so many souls on his shoulders. Fr. Cleopa would later say of his fellow sharer in the monastic mystery:

"One cannot say precisely what the specific gift of Fr. Paisius is. He does not work miracles. He does not preach; no one has heard him preach in church. Neither is he a good chanter; as a celebrant he is not gifted; he has a high-pitched voice, although clear and agreeable. He is sick rather than in good health. At sixty years of age he looked eighty; now he is eighty but looks sixty. He is not a theologian, nor does he hold a diploma or degree in any discipline whatsoever....

"And yet, he has something which captivates. He has

Hieroschema-monk Paisius Olaru.

grace. He has the gift of attracting, of inspiring trust and of always finding the best answers to the most difficult problems and questions. He has warmth and love for men. He opens his door to all. And if someone brings him a gift, he will offer it to the next visitor. He is a very spiritual man, because he is very human. He yearns all the time for silence and solitude, but no one has ever heard him feel sorry for himself because of the noise of so many tourists. The duty of his life is to be 'a man for others.'

"Fr. Paisius is continually being wounded by the sorrows, sufferings, and sicknesses of people, by the multitude of their sins; but at the same time he is serene, full of kindness, indulgent, compassionate, and lenient. Those who go into his cell, on coming out decide to change their lives—they find faith and trust again, and once more center their lives on God and His Word."*

39
Communists Take Over Romania

After Romania had entered World War II on the side of the Allies under the leadership of the reinstated King Michael, Romania agreed to allow military occupation of its territory until a final peace settlement could be reached. This proved to be fatal, since it was the Soviet military that began to occupy Romania. Under the guise of occupation they began to undermine and destabilize King Michael's government. In 1947 King Michael was forced to abdicate. On that very day was announced the creation of the Romanian People's Republic,

* From *Traditsie si Libertate in Spiritualitatea Ortodoxa* by Metropolitan Antonie Plamadeala, pp. 216–18.

under the presidency of the communist dictator Gheorgiu-Dej.*

In 1948 Patriarch Nikodim died under mysterious circumstances. Following his death were the murders of countless hierarchs, priests, monks, nuns, and others who refused to renounce Christ. Prisons were filled with thousands of Christians and others who were seen to be threats to the communist ideology and dictatorial power. Within these prisons the cruelest physical and psychological tortures were conducted. Over the previous forty years the communists in the Soviet Union had made a wicked science of how to destroy a man's will. These unthinkable methods were now employed, especially against the young men in the prisons of Pitesti and Gherla, as the means of forcing a break from Romania's long-standing Christian tradition and forming a "new society."**

40
Fr. Cleopa Escapes into the Wilderness

Thus far, Sihastria had remained untouched in its remote location near the Carpathian Mountains. And, although Abbot Cleopa was only thirty-six years old, he had already become a nationally known spiritual leader of the Christian faith. Now that he had been joined by his spiritual father from his youth, Elder Paisius Olaru, and had the support of Fr. Joel Gheorgiu, Sihastria was fast becoming the spiritual center of Orthodoxy for Romania and thus a threat to the communist government. By the grace that flowed from the eloquent mouth of Fr. Cleopa, a living faith was imparted to those who

* See *The Orthodox Word* no. 155, pp. 343–44.
** This paragraph has been added by the editor.

had ears to hear. The government now sought to dam the flow of faith by stopping Fr. Cleopa from speaking.

In 1948, on May 21, the day that the Church celebrates the memory of the holy Emperor Constantine and Empress Helen, Fr. Cleopa served the Liturgy together with a synaxis of priests and then delivered a sermon which he concluded with the words: "May God grant that today we will have leaders like the holy Emperor and Empress so that the Church will be glorified unto the ages!"

Before he was able to divest himself of his priestly vestments, Fr. Cleopa was seized by the armed Securitate* and forcibly taken away for interrogation. For five days he sat in a cement basement and was continually questioned, while the Securitate shined bright electric lights into his eyes. There was no bed and he was not allowed food or water. Fr. Cleopa would later recall this method of interrogation:

"Later, I asked Fr. Marcu** why they put so many lights in my eyes. I'd put my hands over my eyes so the light would no longer beat down…. It seemed as if it was entering my brain! My brain hurt! They wanted me to lose my memory, so that I'd no longer speak."***

Later he would also reveal to his close disciples how he was able to endure this torture:

"Whoever would enter there would depart nearly crazy. They put me there, too, so that I would lose my mind. I could no longer see with my eyes and could not bear the heat. Then I

---

* The secret police of the communist regime.

**Fr. Marcu Dumutrescu was a courageous confessor who spent many years in prison due to his activity as a Legionaire. In prison he was called "Fakir" because he would never cry out when he was tortured. He also labored with Fr. Cleopa at Slatina and Sihastria monasteries and reposed as a righteous Elder on February 26, 1999.

*** From *Porunca Iubirii (The Commandment to Love)*, no. 6, 1998 (Bucharest: Asociatia Pentru Isihasm).

Fr. Marcu Dumitrescu.

The half-earthen cell of a contemporary desert-dweller in the
wilderness of the Carpathian Mountains.

descended with my mind into my heart with the Prayer of Jesus. After an hour they took me out and were all amazed that I could still speak and move without anyone holding me."

After this scare Fr. Cleopa was released. Someone then came to him secretly and suggested that he go live in the woods and keep out of sight for a while. After consulting with the fathers, Fr. Cleopa withdrew deep into the wilderness, about four miles from the monastery. Here he dug out a hole at the base of a spruce tree and made a half-earthen hut.

Once a week Fr. Macarius would come from the monastery with a little food. Sometimes Fr. Cleopa's old friend from the sheepfold, Fr. Anthony, would bring him provisions. Alone in the wilderness, Fr. Cleopa gave himself over to the practice of the Jesus Prayer and ascetic discipline.

Fr. Cleopa told his disciples that, when he was building

his hut, birds would come and sit on his head. The first time he served Liturgy on a stump in front of his hut, as he was communing the Holy Mysteries, a flock of birds came and gathered, such as he had never seen before. As he gazed upon them in astonishment, he noticed that each one had the sign of the Cross marked on its forehead.

Another time, after reading all the prayers in preparation for Liturgy, he set the Antimension on the tree stump and began the Liturgy with the exclamation, "Blessed is the Kingdom of the Father, and of the Son, and of the Holy Spirit, now and ever, and unto the ages of ages." Again the birds appeared and, as they perched in the branches of the tree, they began to sing in beautiful and harmonic voices. Fr. Cleopa asked himself, "What could this be?" And an unseen voice whispered to him, "These are your chanters on the cliros."

Fr. Cleopa also faced many temptations in the wilderness. Sometimes, while he was asleep, and also while he was awake, he saw demonic apparitions. Regarding that period he related the following:

"One time, at midnight, I was reading my prayer rule and was at the Akathist to the Protection of the Mother of God. All of a sudden a strong rumbling began. 'My,' I said, 'it's a big earthquake!' When I opened the door a little, I saw a large wheel as big as the spruce tree and some hideous creatures surrounding it with pitchforks of fire. One of them said, 'This is the abbot of Sihastria! Put him on the wheel!' And immediately I found myself on the wheel. The wheel was turning and they stood ready with their pitchforks so that, if I fell, I would be impaled on their pitchforks.

"But I had the Akathist book with me and I said, 'Get out of my way! Because I have documents from the Mother of God!' Then I no longer saw the wheel or anything, and I came to myself in the hut."

Each day Fr. Cleopa would read the Akathist to the Protection of the Mother of God. One day, upon opening the book to read, he sensed a fragrance that smelled like lilies and roses. He then prayed to God to remove this fragrance and didn't read the Akathist for a while, realizing that the fragrance was a temptation from the enemy in order to throw him into pride. He would say, "When you pray, it is not good to receive any kind of smell or sensory impressions, because then the demons can come and throw you into pride." When he resumed the reading of the Akathist, he no longer smelled the fragrance. Thus was he delivered from this subtle snare of the devil.

After six months in the wilderness Abbot Cleopa returned again to Sihastria, to the joy of all the monks and the faithful. In 1988, forty years after his first exile into the wilderness, Fr. Cleopa took two disciples to look for the site where he had once lived in his half-earthen hut. For several hours they slowly searched for the site but did not find it. Finally they sat down to rest and eat some food. While they were eating, Fr. Cleopa noticed that they were sitting right next to the site of the hut. The hut had disintegrated by then, but there remained decayed pieces of wood, some tar paper, and a few pieces of iron. Overjoyed to find the place of his spiritual struggles, Fr. Cleopa exclaimed, "Look, a true miracle! When I thought that we'd labored in vain, the Lord made us happy by allowing us to find the cell!" Then, glorifying God, they returned to the monastery.

41

The Renewal of Slatina Monastery

After Fr. Cleopa returned to Sihastria from his exile, a peaceful year passed before he was called to face a new challenge. In August of 1949, by the decree of Patriarch Justinian, Fr. Cleopa was sent with a group of thirty monks to renew Slatina Monastery further north in Bucovina.

Accompanying him was Elder Paisius Olaru together with a synaxis of fathers and brothers. In fulfillment of the prophecy of the righteous Abbot Ioanichie Moroi, Hieroschema-monk Joel Gheorgiu was named abbot "after Cleopa leaves." This division of the brotherhood was painful for all, especially the younger ones who looked to Fathers Cleopa and Paisius for guidance and inspiration. In time, however, the move was a leavening for monastic renewal in the land of Moldavia, Romania.

At the departure of Fathers Cleopa and Paisius, the entire brotherhood accompanied them down the road to send them off and say good-bye. At this moment a spiritual father from the Agapia Convent, Archimandrite Maxim, arrived on the road. Seeing the situation, he offered a comforting word: "Fathers, why are you so sorrowful? The Holy Fathers gave their lives for Christ and defended Orthodoxy, and you holy ones are crying here like the Hebrews by the rivers of Babylon? Hear what the Church sings: 'You holy martyrs who struggled well and were crowned, pray to the Lord that our souls will be saved!' Therefore, be obedient and God will help you through the prayers of the Mother of God!"

Then all joined in chorus to sing "It is Truly Meet ..." and "To Thee the Champion Leader ..." and departed.

At that time Slatina Monastery, which had been founded

Abbot Joel Gheorgiu of Sihastria.

The monastic brotherhood of Slatina (Abbot Cleopa in center).

in 1554 by Alexander Lapusneau,* had only seven elderly monks. Upon arriving, Fr. Cleopa was taken on a tour of the monastery. He was shown the Abbot's quarters and the cells of the brothers, which he blessed with holy water, and finally he was taken to a remote corner of the enclosure to the shop where all the carpentry tools were kept. Fr. Cleopa stopped and joyfully exclaimed, "This will be my cell!"

Overjoyed that God had sent them a capable Abbot, the brothers immediately began to clean up the room. But Fr. Cleopa stopped them, saying, "Brothers, I have no need of help. I will do all that is needed with my own hands," and he himself began working. He put in a bed with simple bedding,

---

* Alexander Lapusneanu was a prince who built Slatina Monastery and many churches throughout Moldavia. He was later tonsured a monk with the name Pachomius.

upon which he laid his sheepskin vest and his many books and letters.

Abbot Cleopa immediately installed the complete cycle of services and daily Liturgy. He also initiated a monastic academy for the brothers, founding the monastic life on the coenobitic model after the rule of St. Theodore the Studite.

After 1950 numerous learned theologians and ascetics who had a special reverence for Fr. Cleopa came to Slatina. Among them were Abbot Petroniu Tanase;* Hierodeacon Anthony Plamadeala, the future Metropolitan of Transylvania; Archimandrite Dositheus Morariu; Protosingul Gerontius Balan; Hieroschema-monk Daniel Tudor;** Hieromonk Arsenius Papacioc;*** and Fr. Marcu Dumitrescu. Thus a unique spiritual community arose, attracting a large number of students, intellectuals, and pilgrims of all ages and classes, who were drawn to Slatina as to a great spiritual magnet.

Abbot Petroniu organized a church choir of over thirty young brothers, which performed the ancient Byzantine chant in a way that reflected the spiritual depth of the monastic community. The Slatina choir was renowned for evoking contrition in the heart of the listener.

---

* Presently abbot of Prodromou Skete on Mt. Athos.

** Known under the pen name of Sandu Tudor, this monk of hesychastic longings was a great national poet and writer. As a brother of Antim Monastery in Bucharest, he was instrumental in founding the Burning Bush Movement. He was arrested twice by the communists. After his first arrest, he composed the Akathist to the Burning Bush. Later, he was abbot of the hesychastic Rarau Skete. This skete could be compared to the skete at Optina Monastery, which he had previously visited.

*** In the world he was a judge and a great sculptor. After laboring with Cornel Codreanu in the Legionaires, he was imprisoned and later emerged as a great spiritual father. He is still alive today.

Fr. Arsenius Papacioc, co-struggler of Fr. Cleopa in the wilderness.

Putna Monastery. One of the monasteries of Moldavia renewed
by Abbot Cleopa.

42
Abbot Cleopa—Renewer of Monastic Life in Moldavia

Within three years Slatina Monastery was a thriving spiritual center for the country of Romania. Knowing that Abbot
Cleopa was at the heart of this success, the chief hierarchs of
Moldavia placed him in charge of overseeing the surrounding
Moldavian monasteries of Putna, Moldovitsa, Rasca, Sihastria,
Rarau, and Sihla. On a regular basis he traveled to each monastery. He placed the main emphasis on obedience with love, the
practice of the Jesus Prayer, and participation in the daily cycle
of services. In addition each monk was given a daily prayer rule
and penances according to the discretion of the confessor.

When any confusion arose Fr. Cleopa sent one or two spiritual fathers in order to restore peace.

In all of these monasteries he established monastic academies so as to sustain a high level of spiritual life.

43
How Abbot Cleopa Was Delivered from the Abbotship of Neamts

At the beginning of 1951 Patriarch Justinian wished to install a similar renewal into the largest monastery of Romania, the Lavra of Neamts. Naturally he thought of Fr. Cleopa.

Hearing this, Fr. Cleopa was greatly saddened and began to pray to the Mother of God to deliver him from this temptation. He remembered the counsel of the righteous ascetic of Agapia, Elder Vincent Malau,* who had once said to him, "Dear boy, when you have great troubles, fast for three days and pray with tears, and God will teach you what to do." So he began a fast. He stayed in his cell fasting not only for three days but for seven. One night he dozed off before the icon of the Mother of God. He saw a heavenly light surround the icon, and then the Mother of God spoke to him through the icon: "Do not be sorrowful about the unrest from Neamts, because I will quiet them down. And do not be doubtful because one thought tells you to go to Neamts and the other to the wilderness."

He then went to Fr. Paisius to confess everything that he had heard and seen from the icon of the Mother of God in his cell. The Elder said to him, "It is a divine sign. But do not tell

* Along with Fr. Ioanichie Moroi, Fr. Vincent Malau (1887–1945) was the most well-known Elder in Romania during the first half of this century. See his Life in *The Orthodox Word* no. 163 (1992).

anyone of this vision for the time being. Now prepare yourself, and tomorrow you will receive Holy Communion. And if it is from God that you go to Neamts Monastery, the Mother of God will help you, and if it is not His will, then you will remain here."

The next day, after the Liturgy, Fr. Cleopa received the news that the Patriarch had consulted with others and had decided that he should remain as abbot of Slatina and overseer of the Moldavian monasteries but not become the abbot of Neamts Lavra, where thousands of pilgrims come each year. Thus, through the protection of the Mother of God and the counsel of his spiritual father, Fr. Cleopa was able to overcome this temptation.

44
Second Flight into the Wilderness
(1952–1954)

Slatina Monastery continued to flourish until 1952. There were now eighty brethren, most of whom were young and zealous. The faithful would come in droves to hear the Holy Liturgy, the prayerful chanting of the monks, and the heart-moving sermons of Abbot Cleopa. Despite the success, Fr. Cleopa still felt that he was away from home. To his close disciples he would say, "I am only here at Slatina in body while in soul I am at Sihastria, where I was tonsured and lived for so many years."

As the spiritual life at Slatina began to shine like a city on a hill, the prince of darkness stirred up his minions in his evil intent to overshadow the light. The Securitate came in force one night and began to interrogate Fr. Cleopa and the better-known monks. When they left they took Fr. Cleopa, Fr. Arsen-

Monastic brothers for life: Fathers Cleopa and Arsenius in old age.

ius Papacioc, and Fr. Marcu Dumitrescu, who was at that time known as Br. Constantine.

At Falticeni they were interrogated all night. They accused Fr. Cleopa, "You have set Bucovina afire with mysticism; you sabotaged the economy of the country. You say, 'Today is George and tomorrow is Basil and it is a feast,' and the people put down their tools and refuse to work! "

In his guileless simplicity Fr. Cleopa answered, "How can I not say it is a feast day if it is written in the calendar of the Holy Church?"

Finally they warned him not to make any "religious propaganda" and let him go.

Returning to Slatina, Fr. Cleopa related all that had happened and, through counsel with the Elders, decided to flee into the wilderness with Fr. Arsenius Papacioc until things quieted down at Slatina. They took with them the Holy Mysteries and hid in the woods near the villages of Neguleasa and Ostra, finding shelter in an abandoned sheepfold. A pious layman named Straton brought them food once a month, and every two or three weeks they partook of the reserved Holy Mysteries which they carried. In this region of the Stanisoara Mountains there was an abundance of wolves. Straton did not fear their attack when he was carrying the food, for he trusted that he would be preserved through the prayers of the two men of God for whose sake he risked his life.

Fr. Cleopa would recall his own encounters with the forest creatures. "When I was in the woods wandering, I'd be examined by my 'friends': Grandpa Bear and Sly Fox. With Grandpa I would get off more easily. When I'd hear him muttering something, I'd throw him a potato and he'd leave, but with the fox it wasn't the same. She'd come up to the door of the hut at night, and if by chance I'd forgotten any food outside, it was her delight. She'd take care of it!

"Once I forgot my cast iron pot in which I cooked my food. It still had something in it. The fox came and, without any shame, began to eat it. I saw her from the window and I went outside. When she saw me, she hurried and the handle of the pot fell over her head. I didn't care so much about the food—I was upset because it was my only pot. I ran after her and cried out, 'Leave the pot!' But a fox always remains a fox—cunning. In her sly way she came up to a branch onto which she hooked the pot, then she ducked her head out and fled. I was happy because she left me my pot!

"I had other, more frightful friends. These were the forest mice and rats. If you weren't organized they would leave you without any food in the dead of winter. I had a bag of rusks tied onto the beam. When night would come, the 'parishioners' would also come out. I didn't care about the rusks they ate but I would get mad because they wouldn't let me do my prayer rule.

"Just as I would begin to read, they'd begin to crunch on the rusks. What should I do? I would take a stick in my right hand and the Psalter in my left. This is how I did my prayer rule: 'Lord, hear my prayer,' and with the stick: 'whack!' after the mice. After I hit them they would pretend to be dead. Then I would continue my supplication and some more verses and then they would begin to crunch again. Again I would hit them with the stick. That is how I did my prayer rule until I plugged up all the holes."

Another time, in late autumn, Fr. Cleopa was hiking through the woods when a cold rain began to pour, which soaked him to the bone. He was still far from his hut and struggled along in his wet clothes. As the wind began to blow, he grew stiff and finally collapsed just a little distance from his hut.

Unable to move, Fr. Cleopa thought, "Now I will die and I don't have the Holy Gifts with me." He prayed fervently, and slowly, very slowly, crawled to his humble shelter. Somehow he managed to thaw his fingers enough to start a fire and revive himself.

Fr. Cleopa also faced more spiritual temptations. "One night I was in the hut. I'd finished the Midnight Office and was at the end of Matins, when all of a sudden I heard, 'Boom, boom, boom!' The earth was shaking! I went outside to see what was happening. When I opened the door of the hut, I saw a great light outside and, in the light, a brass car with many wheels.

"A tall man with big eyes climbed out from it—he was half-white and half-black. He demanded, 'What are you looking for here?' I then remembered what the Holy Fathers say: that if you have the Holy Mysteries, you have the living Christ! I had the Holy Mysteries in the hollow of a spruce tree in the hut. When I realized this, I quickly went inside and with my arms grabbed hold of the spruce tree that had the Holy Mysteries and only said, 'Lord Jesus, do not abandon me!'

"Now, see how intensely one prays when the devil is at the door! When I looked outside again, I saw how the power of Christ drove him back. Near the hut there was a high cliff where the unclean spirit fell. How did he fall? He threw himself headlong down the cliff, with the car and everything, rolling end over end three times on the way down. The noise was so loud that the long and sharp crashing resounded in my ears until one o'clock the next day."

Another time Fr. Cleopa heard a noise outside his hut. When he went outside, it was as if he were in the middle of the war front. He saw tanks coming toward him and armed soldiers walking, and it seemed as if the whole army were trying to capture him. He then began the Jesus Prayer and the apparition disappeared.

Fr. Arsenius would also tell a story about their time in the woods: "Once we were caught together in the woods in a heavy rain. The trees were no higher than a house. Fr. Cleopa was in one area and I was in another. We looked for the thickest covering of bushes in which to shelter ourselves. Father insisted that I come under the branches where he was. I said that my spot was better, which was about thirty yards away from him. But his holiness still insisted, so I said to myself, 'No, wait a minute! I should listen to Fr. Cleopa!' I ran to where he was, and immediately lightning struck right in the spot where I had been. I was deeply affected. Behold the meaning of obedience!"

The winter of 1953 was so cold that Fr. Cleopa was forced to take shelter in the houses of the faithful. In the evenings he would deliver a profitable word to his hosts. Soon the hosts would desire that their relatives and friends also benefit from the soul-profiting discourse of the monk. Before long a big crowd would congregate, and then Fr. Cleopa would secretly depart, leaving a note: "I have left. Forgive me." And he would return to the mountains.

Fathers Cleopa and Arsenius struggled in a life of deprivation and hardship in the Stinsoara Mountains until the summer of 1954, when Patriarch Justinian obtained approval for the two ascetics to return either to the monastery or to the Patriarchate. When they came to take him down, he was afraid that perhaps it was a trap. He began to pray to God to reveal if he should or should not go. Then the words of St. John of the Ladder came to his mind, "It is a disgrace for a shepherd to fear death, because the definition of obedience is fearlessness of death." With this in mind he asked himself, "Who is calling me? The Patriarch of the Church is calling me! If he sends me to death, I will go to death!"

Thus, after well over two years of hermitic struggles, Fathers Cleopa and Arsenius departed the wilderness to Bucharest accompanied by Hieroschema-monk Daniel Tudor. They were received with love by Patriarch Justinian, with whom they met each night for spiritual converse. They also visited many of the monasteries in the capital, where they confessed and gave guidance to the monks. Soon thereafter the fathers returned to Slatina Monastery, to the joy of the brethren and all the faithful.*

---

* Fr. Arsenius Papacioc and Fr. Marcu Dumitrescu were arrested at Slatina Monastery in 1958, a few years after Fr. Cleopa and Fr. Arsenius hid in the woods. At the end of Matins, in the early hours of the morning when they left the church, there were eighty-nine soldiers waiting to arrest them! Fr. Arsenius said to them, "The mountains shook with fear, and out came a mouse! Why all the theatrics!? If you had called me on the telephone, I would have come."

45
Monastic Revival

At the beginning of 1956 Archimandrite Cleopa was freed from his duty as abbot of Slatina Monastery, leaving his disciple Emilian Olaru as his replacement. Fr. Cleopa was called to go on a spiritual mission to Timisoara and Arad, accompanied by two disciples. Here he was met by the Metropolitan of Banat, Basil Lazarescu, who had just prepared a reliquary for the relics of St. Joseph the New of Partos.*

Fr. Cleopa then visited Vasiova Monastery, where for many years had served the righteous Fr. Vincent Malau, who had once given the young Br. Constantine soul-saving words of advice. The missionary Abbot then went on to Gai Monastery near Arad, where he installed the Sihastria typicon. However, when the bell was rung at midnight for Matins, the local inhabitants, not being accustomed to services at that hour, called the fire department, thinking that the monastery had caught on fire. Fr. Cleopa used the opportunity to call everyone into church and deliver a soul-stirring sermon in which he exclaimed, "The fire which has been set aflame here in Gai Monastery—may it not be extinguished until the end of the world!"

---

* St. Joseph lived in the sixteenth and seventeenth centuries and spent much of his monastic life on Mt. Athos in Pantocrator Monastery. In his later life he became a desert-dweller in the surrounding wilderness, where he performed miracles and healed the sick. He was called out from his wilderness to be the spiritual father of his community and later abbot of Koutloumousiou Monastery, and eventually he retired to Vatopedi Monastery. At the age of eighty he was called out of retirement to be Metropolitan of Timisoara in Romania. Three years later he reposed, in 1656. He was canonized in 1956.

Indeed, everywhere Fr. Cleopa went a monastic renewal and zeal for the Christian life spread like wildfire. After visiting other monasteries in that region, Fr. Cleopa returned to Moldavia and settled at Putna Monastery for several months, where he instructed the monks in the spiritual life. He left at Putna Archimandrite Dositheus Morariu, who had once been a disciple of Abbot Ioanichie Moroi and who was soon elected abbot of Putna.

Although this was at a time when many were imprisoned and put to death for speaking about Christianity, and although Fr. Cleopa himself had been personally threatened, he would fearlessly speak to the local pilgrims with great enthusiasm about the right-believing ruler Prince Stephen Voda of Moldavia. With great courage and self-sacrifice Prince Stephen had defended the land and the Right Faith, and had built numerous churches, which stand to the present day. During his stay Fr. Cleopa had the opportunity to speak to the youth and the older generation, to Romanians and to foreigners, about the beauty of Orthodoxy, the heroism of Romania's forebears, the artistic treasures of Romania's frescoed churches, the glory of God, and the blessings of the Romanian nation. In these sermons Fr. Cleopa articulated the harmony between Romania's Orthodox piety and the patriotism of its forebears, as well as the sacrifice of generations of monks who kept aflame the lamp of Orthodoxy and thus the soul of the Romanian nation.

In the autumn of 1956 Fr. Cleopa donned his sheepskin coat, gathered his spiritual books which he so loved, and returned to the monastery of his repentance, to the holy Sihastria Monastery. At that time the monastery was still under the guidance of Abbot Joel Gheorgiu, the former cell-attendant of Abbot Ioanichie Moroi.

46
Sihastria (1949–1959)

Fr. Cleopa's successor as abbot of Sihastria, the humble Fr. Joel Gheorgiu, guided the community with great wisdom for ten years. Attending all the church services, he was the first to enter the church and the last to leave. When he would see a brother or father coming late to church, he would say, "Dear Father, come on time to church! Do not miss the holy services if you are not busy with an obedience because that is why we came to the monastery!" In his zeal and love for the house of God, he was a burning icon for all the brethren. Along with Fr. Paisius Olaru, who returned from Slatina in 1953, he was the spiritual father for the entire community. Together, the Elders maintained the spiritual life of the monastery at the level to which Fr. Cleopa had raised it before his departure to Slatina; and Sihastria Monastery continued to attract new young monastic aspirants.

With Fr. Cleopa's return, the spiritual life at the monastery was strengthened even more. Fr. Cleopa began living in a cell on a hill near the monastery, where he would receive the faithful, while Fr. Paisius, being a lover of silence, stayed in a cell in the woods, where he confessed his spiritual children. Abbot Joel continued to attend all the services in the monastery church and occupied the abbot's quarters. Thus, each in his own way, advancing in prayer and grace, offered a unique dynamic to the community and prepared the brethren to face the difficult trials looming on the horizon. Fr. Paisius would urge his disciples to a life of silence and prayer. Fr. Cleopa would urge all—monks and laymen—not to forget the hour of death, to obey one's spiritual father in all things, and to defend

Fr. Paisius Olaru, Fr. Cleopa, and Fr. Joel Gheorgiu.

the Orthodox Faith in and out of season. Finally, Abbot Joel called all to constancy in attending the divine services.

The period between 1956 and 1959 was a time of spiritual development granted by God not only for Sihastria but for nearly all the monasteries of Romania. This was allowed so that the Christian Faith would be prepared to withstand another wave of persecution from the communist regime, which had now been in power for over a decade. Thus the Romanian Orthodox Church would continue the destiny of the Apostolic Church: to be continually persecuted yet protected from on high, strengthened by the blood of the martyrs.

47
Persecution (1959–1964)

April of 1959 marked the beginning of the most difficult time for Romanian monasticism in the twentieth century. Nearly all the abbots and spiritual fathers were banished from their monasteries, together with all the novices and ryassa-phore monks and nuns. The attempt was thus made to sever the bond between spiritual father and disciple in the atheists' drive to destroy the people's faith.

Toward the end of 1959 a decree was passed by the atheist government in Bucharest that all monks under the age of fifty-five and all nuns under fifty were to be barred from all monasteries. This decree was enforced by the armed and violent Securitate together with the political authorities in each region. In less than one year, over four thousand monks and nuns were exiled from their monasteries.

Due to the spiritual wealth of Moldavia, its monasteries were hit the hardest. Sihastria and Slatina were turned into old-age homes for elderly monastics. Smaller sketes remained without monks, while missionary monasteries were turned into parishes under lay priests. No new monastic aspirants were allowed.

Some of the exiled monks formed secret monastic households in the region they were assigned, while many others fled into the wilderness. Others—some of whom had taken their vows and some of whom had not—married and returned to the world. It was a time of testing.

The Abbot of Sihastria, Fr. Joel, and Hieromonk Barsanuphius Lipan were both banished to their native villages on April 22, 1959. Sihastria lost forty monks under the age of fifty-five and its Abbot. Fr. Cleopa lost the majority of his spiritual sons, including his cell-attendant.

48
Fr. Cleopa's Third Exile to the Wilderness

For the third time Fr. Cleopa was led by the Spirit into the mountains of Moldavia, to his much-beloved silence. He began his sojourn near the village of Hangu, from where he went northwards by way of Mount Halauca-Pipirig, until he reached a spot near the summit of Petru-Voda Mountain. There he built a small wooden hut in which he lived for two years, being helped by a devoted Christian in that region by the name of Paul Marin.

In 1962, after two years alone, Fr. Cleopa was joined by his close disciple Fr. Barsanuphius. Together they labored in asceticism in numerous places for well over three years. They would confess to each other weekly and would commune of the Holy Mysteries which were brought from Sihastria every two or three weeks. The fathers were assisted at this time by Dumitru Nita and George Olteanu from Dolhesti, as well as by the relatives of Fr. Barsanuphius.

Fr. Cleopa and his cell-attendant Fr. Barsanuphius, who became
Fr. Cleopa's confessor after the death of Elder Paisius Olaru.

During this period in the solitude of the mountains, Fr.
Cleopa further developed his inward life of prayer. Each day he
would devote between ten and twelve hours to prayer in soli-
tude. According to Fr. Barsanuphius, in the morning he was
accustomed to pray the following: Morning Prayers, several
Akathists (which always included the ones to the Lord Jesus
Christ and the Annunciation of the Mother of God), the
Canon of Repentance, the Canon to the Guardian Angel, the
Canon to the Heavenly Powers, and then a portion out of the
Psalter. After noon he would read Vespers and Compline with
the Canon to the Mother of God. Then he would take his only
meal of the day, after which he would continue his prayer rule
with the Evening Prayers and the Paraclesis to the Mother of
God. The remaining time he would devote to the Jesus Prayer.
Fr. Barsunuphius also attested that Fr. Cleopa had acquired the
Prayer of the Heart to such a degree that he would weep ardent

tears and would feel a great spiritual warmth in his heart, which would burn like a blazing fire.

Another fruit of this desert silence and continual prayer was the series of writings that Fr. Cleopa composed at this time. Between the times of prayer, Fr. Cleopa would sit under a spruce tree and write. During the five years of his third exile Fr. Cleopa wrote the following books: *Ascent toward Resurrection* (sermons for monks), *Confession for Bishops*, *Confession for Abbots*, *Confession for Spiritual Fathers*, *Confession for Lay Priests*, *Confession for Monks*, *About Dreams and Visions*, and *The Miracles of God in His Creation*.

49
Sihastria during Fr. Cleopa's Absence

After the exile of Abbot Joel and Fr. Cleopa, the guidance of the spiritual life of the monks and pilgrims who came to Sihastria fell to the aging Elder Paisius. During this time of monastic persecution, serving priests were few, spiritual fathers were rare, and the young ones desiring monastic life were kept in workers' clothes so as not to attract the attention of the Securitate.

All who came to Sihastria wondered about Fr. Cleopa and greatly missed his fatherly presence and consoling words. The faithful felt the hidden power of his prayer and all believed that he would again return to his flock. In the meantime his devoted spiritual children prayed continually for him.

The new Abbot of Sihastria was Fr. Caliopie Apetri, a disciple of Fr. Cleopa, who had been with him during his time in Slatina. He was courageous, bold and zealous for that which is holy and full of goodness. He maintained the same typicon during the time of persecution and ruled the monastery for twelve years. Finally, the situation began to improve in 1963.

50
The Tears of Mother Agafia

[The following story is told by the author, Fr. Ioanichie Balan, about Fr. Cleopa's mother, the Nun Agafia:]

"I had come from Targu Neamts to Sihastria Monastery through Old Agapia. I had wanted to console Fr. Cleopa's mother and to bring her some necessities. When I arrived at the gate of the monastery, the elderly Mother Agafia was waiting for any pilgrim to arrive in order to talk with him. When she would see someone entering the enclosure of the monastery, Mother Agafia, without knowing him, would ask, 'Excuse me. Have you seen my Cleopa?' The believer would say, 'No, Mother, I do not know him!'

"When other believers would come to worship, the old one would come close to them and ask them with tears in her eyes, 'Have you somehow seen my Cleopa?' And they would answer, 'We don't know where he is, Mother. We haven't seen him!' Then the old one would sigh and would wipe the tears from her eyes, looking off somewhere in the distance.

"Understanding her great pain, I drew near to Mother Agafia and gave her the things I had prepared for her and said to her meekly, 'Mother Agafia, do not ask people anymore where Fr. Cleopa is, because they do not know where he is to be found.'

"Then the old one said to me with tears of pain, 'Oh, Fr. Ioanichie, you do not know what it means to be a mother!'

"Her words were full of tears, and after I venerated in the church, I said, 'Let it be, Mother Agafia, because soon Fr. Cleopa will come to Sihastria Monastery.' Then I departed over the mountain to the monastery.

Fr. Cleopa with his disciple and the author of this biography,
Fr. Ioanichie Balan.

"In the afternoon of the next day, Mother Agafia, seized with longing for her son Cleopa, took her stick in hand and without saying a word to the mothers started out across the mountains toward Sihastria. But, being alone and over eighty-eight years old, she lost the trail in the woods. Toward evening she found a man and he brought her to a forest cabin. She did not know how to return or how to make it to Sihastria. The workers at the cabin gave her a room to sleep in for the night. During this time the bells of Agapia Monastery were being rung continually and all the sisters were looking for her in the woods. It was not until the afternoon of the second day that they found her. 'How did you get here, Mother Agafia?' they asked.

"'I wanted to go to Sihastria to see if my Cleopa had come, but I got lost. A man brought me to this hut and I didn't know where to go.'

"'Come with us, Mother Agafia.'

"Arriving at Sihastria, Mother Agafia fell to her knees before the graves of her two sons, Basil and Gerasim. After she had wept sufficiently, she got up and kissed the crosses, venerated in the church, and said to the sisters: 'Now I can die! But won't you let me stay here?'

"'No Mother Agafia. Let's go back!'

"'Let's go....'"

51
The Return of Fr. Cleopa

In August of 1964 a general amnesty was given by the communist government to all political prisoners. As the prisons were emptied of their surviving prisoners, the monasteries were once again allowed to carry on in freedom. A wave of joy swept across the country because of the newly gained freedom.

Prayers of thanksgiving were offered up in monasteries and churches.

[It was Fr. Ioanachie Balan of Sihastria who was chosen to bring the glad tidings to Fr. Cleopa, who was still hiding in the woods. Fr. Ioaniche recalls:]

"I arrived at the hut of Fr. Cleopa, whose location was unknown to most. Falling to my knees, I kissed his hand. We embraced one another and wept together. It seemed as if I were dreaming. Then the Lord strengthened us and we prayed for a long time, and I said to Fr. Cleopa, 'Most Holy Father, I came, sent by the fathers of Sihastria, to bring you home after almost six years of separation. They have opened the prisons and God has blessed the country with a little freedom. Thus, we ask you to return to Sihastria! All the fathers are waiting for you and weeping for joy. The faithful are also waiting, but the ones who want you the most are Fr. Paisius, the spiritual father of us all, who raised you since you were small, and Mother Agafia, your holiness's mother.'

"Fr. Cleopa hesitated. He had become accustomed to the silence. A battle was going on in his soul. Should he renounce his silence for the benefit of others or remain in his prayerful life in the wilderness? Seeing him in this conflict, I left him to pray to God for two more weeks. On September 29, the day of St. Cyriacus the Hesychast, Fr. Cleopa, together with his disciple Barsanuphius, traversed the mountains and valleys, through the woods known only to them, until they arrived at Sihastria Monastery.*

---

* Fr. Barsanuphius remained one of the closest disciples of Fr. Cleopa. After the death of Elder Paisius Olaru he was Fr. Cleopa's confessor, until he himself reposed in 1997. At his deathbed Fr. Cleopa read the prayers for the departure of the soul, and as he pronounced the words, 'Give rest to him where the souls of the righteous are,' the obedient disciple breathed twice and gave his soul into the hands of God.

The mountain pass across which Fr. Cleopa travelled on his return to
Sihastria after his final sojourn in the wilderness.

The brotherhood of Sihastria after Fr. Cleopa's return. 1970.

"The joy was great. The fathers and brothers kissed him with tears in their eyes and gave glory to God that once again he had returned healthy to his cell. In thanksgiving, that night we celebrated an All-night Vigil. Fr. Cleopa spent the following day with his spiritual father, Hieroschema-monk Paisius."

52
The Good Shepherd

The news of Fr. Cleopa's return to Sihastria spread in a few days throughout the entire country. Again he began to pastor the people. More and more each day, the faithful, both from Moldavia and from outside its borders, would come to receive a profitable word, to confess their sins, and to pray at the holy monastery. At times he would receive over a hundred people a day at his cell. They would listen to his counsels and words of encouragement and ask him spiritual and theological questions. Both the most simple and the most educated would depart from him pleased. Across the nation he was seen as a heavenly blessing and a hero of Orthodoxy for the Romanian people.

The Elder's self-acquired learning and God-given power of speech were not meant to be hidden under a bushel, or even to remain within Orthodox circles. In 1990 a group of Protestants from the West rented a stadium in Suceava and challenged any representative of Orthodoxy to a public debate. Little did they know about the monk who received his theological education at the sheepfold—a man with such an astounding memory and a thorough knowledge of Scripture that it seemed he was born to preach the Gospel. At the request of the faithful, Elder Cleopa accepted the challenge and thoroughly defeated the Protestants.*

---

* *The Orthodox Word* no. 162 (1992), p. 16.

Elder Cleopa visiting the sheepfold where he spent his formative
years in monastic life.

The first duty which the Elder required of all the faithful—from whatever station of life they came—was to keep to
the dogmas of the Orthodox Faith. Then he would emphasize
the confession of sins, urging all to confess at least four times a
year. He would say, "Brother, when you see that your father or
mother have become ill, don't call the doctor first, but call the
priest. Because the doctor can't give him a moment of life.
Even if he could, he wouldn't give it to you, but he'd keep it for
himself. All is how God wants it. Call the priest and say to
him, 'Father, stay here and hear my father's or mother's complete confession.'

"He who confesses should tell everything he has done.
Because if we don't err in deeds, we err with the mind or by
word. And the priest, at the end, can absolve him from all sins
by the grace which Christ has given to him.

"Then you can also call the doctor. Because if the man dies having confessed everything, the Church can pull him out of hell in forty days or possibly more. But if he is unconfessed and has grave sins, not even the services can pull him out of hell. There is no salvation without confession."

Fr. Cleopa recommended that each have his confessor in his own parish. If someone desired a more detailed confession, he could confess to an elder at a monastery. In this case, he would have to receive a blessing from his priest before going to the monastery.

In addition to many pilgrims, Fr. Cleopa himself would confess approximately forty of the monks of Sihastria and many monks and nuns from other monasteries, as well as lay priests and hierarchs, including two Patriarchs. Through confession Fr. Cleopa would gain many souls for Christ. He would ask each one to fulfill a penance which he would give. If someone said he could not fulfill it, he would give him a smaller penance according to his zeal and strength.

He asked each believer to pray much, even as the Apostle Paul commanded the faithful to *pray without ceasing* (I Thess. 5:17). In general he gave the following rule: Morning Prayers, the Akathist to the Mother of God and, in the evening, Prayers before Sleep and the Paraclesis to the Mother of God with candles lit. For the rest of the day, he would urge all to repeat the Jesus Prayer.

In calling others to constant prayer, Fr. Cleopa was the first fulfiller of this commandment. He would daily pray for himself, for the Church, for the faithful, for those fallen into grave sins, for the sick, and for the suffering. Indeed, the power of Fr. Cleopa's prayer at times performed true miracles. Those for whom he prayed would return healthy from the hospital and safely from journeys, and would succeed in their exams and in daily life.

Once a believing woman came with her husband to Fr. Cleopa in a state of desperation because three of her bosses at work were preparing to fire her unjustly. After she explained the situation, the Elder comforted her with these words: "Do not be afraid. You will come to me and you will tell me, 'Father, I have never seen such a miracle!'"

The woman went home at peace but her difficulties at work became worse. She was just about to be fired. Her husband had lost his patience and trust, and did not want to go back to the monastery again, when all of a sudden the miracle that had been foretold occurred.

Over the course of the week all three of her bosses were fired: on Monday, the highest-ranking one; on Wednesday, the next one in line; and on Friday the last one was fired. When they visited Fr. Cleopa again, both the man and his wife cried out involuntarily, "Father, we have never seen such a miracle!"

He would call the faithful to go to church every week or, in case of need, two to three times a week. When the whole family could not go together, he told them to send one person in their family, who would be named the "Apostle of the Family." He instructed those staying at home to read holy books, to pray, and not to eat until the "Apostle of the Family" had returned from church with the holy bread.

Fr. Cleopa urged everyone to acts of mercy: "Do not let anyone depart from you without alms! If you don't have money, give him a potato, a piece of bread, a handkerchief, or give him a little something. If you give a little and you are sorry that you can't give more, your acts of mercy reach God like lightning. Why? Two great virtues are met: almsgiving and humility."

He would counsel each one to do acts of mercy in the name of Christ according to his strength, because he who gives alms "gives to God" and is more easily saved. As the Lord says

A profitable word.

in the Holy Scripture, *Blessed are the merciful, for they shall obtain mercy* (Matt. 5:7).

Fr. Cleopa called the faithful to live in permanent love and Christian harmony, according to the word of Christ Himself, *By this will all men know that you are My disciples, if you have love one to another* (John 13:35).

In regard to family life, he recommended that young people live in virginity until they are married in the Church, and that they be obedient to their priests and parents, according to the command given by Moses: *Honor thy father and thy mother, that thy days may be long upon the land* (Ex. 20:12). He strictly forbade abortions, as one of the most severe sins. For those who had lawsuits and quarrels over earthly things, the Elder would ask them to reconcile with one another and to follow the counsel of their priests.

Finally, Fr. Cleopa would end by giving a profitable word

in accord with his listeners' understanding and would answer questions. He would bless them with the holy cross and anoint them, give them little icons and incense, and dismiss them in peace to their homes. After he had had a short rest, another group of the faithful would come seeking his counsel and blessing. In the summer he would have many groups numbering hundreds of people. He continued this mission from the fall of 1964 until December 2, 1998, when he gave his spirit into the hands of God.

53
Uncreated Light

Many were the variously colored stars who shone forth in asceticism under the guidance of the great luminary of Romanian monasticism in the twentieth century, Elder Cleopa. Between the years 1968 and 1970 there were, in particular, two elderly monks who would remain in church after the Matins service. After everyone had left, they would lie outstretched on the floor of the church in the form of the Cross and begin to pray with tears to the Savior asking for mercy, forgiveness, and absolution of sins. It was the priest from Ghindaoani, Fr. Dumitru Bejan,* who discovered their ascetic labor during one of his visits to Sihastria.

The two elderly monks, unaware of anyone's presence in

---

* Fr. Dumitru Bejan was born in 1909 and ordained a priest in 1938. He was imprisoned by the Soviets between 1942 and 1948 and was placed in many prison camps including Karaganda. When he returned to Romania he was again arrested and put in the camps for seven more years (from 1949 to 1956). After three more years of forced exile, he was again imprisoned. Fr. Dumitru was a bold confessor who never once compromised his faith. He wrote books on his prison experience, out of which he emerged as a great spiritual light. He reposed in 1995.

church, lay with their faces to the ground and began to pray from the heart. As Fr. Dumitru watched them pray, to his amazement he saw a translucent flame of light rise and intensify over their heads. Seeing this flame of the grace of the Holy Spirit manifest, Fr. Dumitru fell to his knees and joined the two elders in prayer.

After a little time the flame of grace slowly diminished until it finally dissipated. Then the two old ones got up on their feet, made three prostrations, and venerated the holy icons, and each departed for his own cell.

Behold, even in our times there are still monks of holy life who have the gift of fiery prayer. The names of these two monks are not known up to today, but some of the Elders say that they were the Fathers Januarius and Cassian, disciples of Elder Cleopa. However, this remains a mystery of God.

54
Woman of Prayer

Elder Cleopa told the following story about an incident that occurred in the church of Sihastria:

"In the winter of 1971 it was my turn to serve at the Holy Altar. I came to the church at four in the morning to say my prayers before Holy Communion in front of the Holy Table. After not much time had passed, a woman entered to pray. She had come to the monastery the previous evening. I did not know her. She prayed slowly before all the icons and was constantly making prostrations. She did not know that there was someone else in the church, since it was dark, being wintertime. Seeing that she was praying so diligently, I looked through the Holy Doors to see who was praying with so much faith. The woman was on her knees in the middle of the church with her hands raised and was saying from her whole heart these words: 'Lord, do not leave me! Lord, do not leave me!'

"Then I saw a yellowish light around her head and it frightened me terribly. The woman fell with her face to the ground and prayed voicelessly. The ray of light above her became bigger and rose above her head. After a little time the light slowly went out. The woman got up and went out of the church. It was a peasant woman.

"Behold who has the gift of prayer! Behold, lay people surpass us monks! I had finished Proskomedia, and with great feeling I began to weep with the spear in my hand. Only God knows how many chosen ones there are in the world!"

55
Pilgrimage to the Holy Land

[Fr. Ioanichie Balan recalls his pilgrimage with Fr. Cleopa:]

"In the fall of 1974, ten years after Fr. Cleopa's return from the wilderness, many pilgrims from the country, together with Fr. Cleopa and Fr. Joel Gheorgiu, departed for the Holy Land and worshipped at the Sepulchre of the Lord and the other holy places.

"This was one of the greatest joys in Fr. Cleopa's life. The first and holiest road on which we walked was on the way to worship at the Sepulchre of the Lord in the holy walled city of Jerusalem. We then climbed Golgotha and kissed the Holy Cross, upon which Christ was crucified for our salvation and for the whole world. There we listened to the Holy Liturgy, and, giving glory to our Savior Jesus Christ, we went on pilgrimage to the other places in Jerusalem, with our souls full of joy and tender feeling.

"During the following days we worshipped on Mt. Zion, where the Mother of God fell asleep, as well as at the tomb of the Prophet David. Then we went down into the Garden of Gethsemane and worshipped at the tomb of the Mother of God and all the holy places there. With the New Testament in hand we climbed to the Mount of Olives and stopped at two big Orthodox women's monasteries: St. Mary Magdalen and Ascension, where ten Romanian nuns labor in asceticism.

"So we roamed through the Holy Land up to Galilee, to the town of Nazareth, where the Mother of God received the news of the Incarnation of Christ. Fr. Cleopa, who had tasted so many of the sorrows of this life, was rejoicing the most among us.

"We made other stops in the town of Cana of Galilee and at the well of the Samaritan woman. From there we arrived at the Jordan River, in which Christ, the Savior of the world, was baptized, and we returned to Jerusalem.

"Then we departed toward Bethlehem, the town where Christ the Lord was born. We tarried for a day, asking the Savior to also be spiritually born in our hearts and souls.

"After a few days we all departed on a journey of 186 miles to Mt. Sinai, on which Moses received the Tablets of the Law. Moses led the chosen people from here to the Holy Land. Lord, what a wilderness this place is and how blessed is our country, Romania, shaded and protected in Thy great goodness!

"On the horizon could be seen, like an invincible fortress, the monastery of St. Catherine, where there are found relics of the great martyrs. Here we were received with much graciousness by Metropolitan Damianos, the Abbot of the monastery.

"On the next day we climbed to the summit of the mountain where the holy Prophet Moses received the Tablets of the Law. We then returned to the Holy City of Jerusalem, giving glory to God for everything.

"After we worshipped again at the Sepulchre of the Lord, we visited the village of Ain Karem, the birthplace of St. John the Baptist, then Jericho and the monasteries in the Jordan Valley. On October 30 we returned to Romania."

56
Pilgrimage to Mt. Athos

[Fr. Ioanichie continues:] "Three years after the first pilgrimage, in September 1977, a group of four fathers from Sihastria Monastery, headed by Archimandrite Cleopa Ilie, departed by train toward Mt. Athos.

"Athos, called the 'Garden of the Mother of God' is the second holiest place in the Christian world, after the Sepulchre of the Lord. Athos is the paradise of Orthodox lands, unique in the Christian world.

"We arrived at Thessalonica, the capital of ancient Macedonia, where we met with some Romanian monks. For a whole day we visited the old churches and monasteries of northern Greece, after which we left for Mt. Athos.

"On the horizon we could see some Athonite monasteries, the port of Daphne, and the peak of Athos, over six thousand feet. It all seemed like a divine miracle. Mt. Athos is a narrow strip of land with a surface area of 130 square miles, over 50 miles long, which houses twenty large monasteries, over fifteen sketes, and about two hundred cells, large and small, in which over fifteen hundred Greek, Serbian, Russian, Romanian and Bulgarian monks labor in asceticism.

"After two hours of traveling by boat, we got out at the Port of Daphne and climbed toward Karyes, the capital of the Holy Mountain. After obtaining an entry visa into Mt. Athos,

Archimandrite Cleopa and pilgrims with Romanian brethren
at Prodromou Skete, Mt. Athos.

we started out toward the Romanian Skete, Prodromou, where
we stayed for two days. Saturday night, at the service of Matins, Ryassaphore Monk John, a disciple of Fr. Cleopa, was tonsured into monasticism under Fr. Cleopa's mantle. The tonsure
was officiated by Archimandrite Victorin, the Abbot of Sihastria Monastery, who gave him the name Ioanichie.

"Then the Holy Liturgy was celebrated and Fr. Cleopa
uttered a beautiful sermon. After the meal we visited all the
caves and cells of the desert-dwellers around Prodromou Skete,
and on the next day we departed to worship in the
world-famous Athonite monasteries.

"The first stop we made was at the Monastery of the
Great Lavra. Here we venerated at the tomb of St. Athanasius
the Athonite in the narthex of the church.

"Afterwards we visited the Romanian kellion of Lacu
Skete and Iveron Monastery, Koutloumousiou and Stav-

ronikita, all of which were restored by Moldavian and Montenian rulers who had donated money year after year. What moved us most was the icon of the Mother of God, called 'Portaitissa,'* at Iveron Monastery, where we all venerated with Elder Cleopa at our head. On the way toward Karyes we made a short stop at the cell of the renowned hesychast, Paisios the Athonite, a great holy man, honored and sought out in the whole of Greece, who amazed us with his holiness and humility.

"The cell of Fr. Paisios in Capsala is surrounded by grape vineyards. We knocked at the gate and waited. A monk small of stature, thin, modestly clothed, about seventy-five years of age, but luminous of face and full of humility, came and opened the gate for us. It was the Elder!

"'Bless us, Fr. Paisios! We are pilgrims from Romania.'

"'The Lord bless us all!'

"He invited us into a small chapel next to the cell, where we venerated and sang the Axion to the Mother of God. Then he invited us into his cell for guests, about eight by twelve feet. We sat down. There were about ten of us in all. Fr. Paisios served us, according to the custom of Athonite monks, with sweets and cold water. Then he sat on a small chair on the threshold of the door.

"'Fr. Paisios, we come from far away. Please—give us a profitable word.'

"'Forgive me, please. I am not a hieromonk and I do not dare to give a profitable word to priests,' answered the Elder.

"'Nevertheless, find for us a profitable word.'

"'Fathers, I have not yet finished the school of monasticism and I don't know many words.'

"Seeing his humility, Archimandrite Cleopa asked him,

---

* "One Who Stands at the Gate," i.e., Protectress of Mt. Athos.

Elder Paisios the New of Mount Athos (1924–1994).

'Fr. Paisios, which prayer is more beneficial for a monk: to read the Psalter or to say the Jesus Prayer?'

"'Both are good,' he answered, 'only say them from the heart, with faith and with tears.'

"'Which monastic ascetical labor is better? Common life or that of the wilderness [desert-dwelling]?'

"'If you have humility,' the Elder said, 'in either you can be saved. He who wants to be sure of salvation enters into a community under obedience; and he who loves stillness and prayer more withdraws in solitude.'

"'How can we help in the salvation of others?'

"'Through prayer. The monk is first of all a man of prayer and a candle on a candlestand for everyone. Only in this way can we help and spiritually build up people. First is prayer, then the example of our life, then the word of instruction.'

"'How can we obtain the gift of tears?'

"'If we have the humility of the saints, we will obtain both the Prayer of the Heart and the gift of tears. I haven't been able to obtain this gift, which is received from God by great labor.'

"'What opinion do you have of Athonite monasticism today?'

"'I don't have any opinion. But I know that all came to the Holy Mountain to glorify God and to be saved. Thus all force themselves, according to their zeal and their strength, in prayer, in obedience, in fasting, in nightly vigils, and in all good works. All humble themselves, have hope, and labor and follow Christ. Who, however, will lay hold of the crown of salvation, no one knows except God alone.'

"'What books must monastics read?'

"'First of all the Holy Scriptures. Then the *Lives of Saints* and the Patristic writings. We do not have to read or speak a lot, but we must do a lot!'

"'Fr. Paisios, how many times must we partake of Holy Communion per year?'

"'The promptings of the heart and our spiritual father indicate to us how many times. Some more often, others less often. But if monastics can commune once a week, it is very good. Lay people—less frequently and in accordance with what their spiritual fathers decide.'

"'What other counsel can you give us?'

"'Let us always be ready for death because we *know neither the day nor the hour wherein the Son of man cometh* (Mt. 25:13).

"'Fr. Paisios, how many hours must a monk sleep at night?'

"'If I added up how many hours I sleep lying down on a bed and how many I sleep on my feet, you would see that I sleep all day long, because I do not keep watch with my mind in prayer!'

"And we, benefiting greatly from the humility and wisdom of Fr. Paisios, thanked him for receiving us and for the counsel given, asked for his blessing, and continued on our way.*

"Then we went to the miracle-working icons at the Protaton in Karyes, and at the Pantocrator, Esphigmenou, and Vatopedi Monasteries, where many relics and some miracle-working icons are to be found. Stephen the Great** constructed a harbor at Vatopedi, which has been maintained in good condition until today.

---

* This interview is from *Pelerinaj la Muntele Athos* by Archimandrite Ioanichie Balan, pp. 116–18.
** Stephen the Great was a ruler of Moldavia in the fifteenth century who defended the Moldavian land for half a century after the fall of Byzantium. He won forty-seven battles and built forty-eight churches. His spiritual father was St. Daniel the Hesychast. King Stephen was canonized by the Romanian Orthodox Church in 1992.

"We continued our pilgrimage to Chilandar Monastery. From there we crossed the hills and stopped at Zographou Monastery, which was built from the foundation by Stephen the Great between 1475 and 1502. The patronal feast of the monastery is the feast of St. George.

"We worshipped then at the monasteries on the western side of Mt. Athos, namely, Docheiariou Monastery (founded entirely by Alexandru Lapusneanu in the sixteenth century), Xenophont and Panteleimon Monasteries, and the monasteries of Xeropotamou, Simonopetra (founded by Michael the Brave),* Philotheou, Gregoriou (founded by Stephen the Great), Dionysiou (founded by Neagoe Basarab),** and St. Paul.

"When the Athonite abbots heard of the coming of Archimandrite Cleopa to Mt. Athos, a good number of them solicited him to speak a profitable word to the brothers of their monasteries. Thus he delivered five spiritual sermons with Patristic and exceptional Philokalic content, which consoled many young souls. Many were published and made an impact throughout all of Greece.

"Leaving the Holy Mountain of Athos, we visited Athens and the monasteries in its vicinity, and we went to the great spiritual father, Porphyrius, who had the gift of clairvoyance. A true saint of our days! He labored in a small skete in Attica.

---

* Michael the Brave was a ruler of Moldavia and builder of churches. After Byzantium fell to the Turks, it was the rulers of Moldavia, Wallachia, and Transylvania (what is today known as Romania) who took up the cause of promoting hesychastic monasticism by supporting monasteries on Mt. Athos as well as in their native land.

** Neagoe Basarab was a ruler of Wallachia from 1512 to 1521. He was the greatest builder of churches in the sixteenth century. "A friend of letters" and "a man of culture," he sought to reach the ideal of a "hesychast monarch." His spiritual father, Patriarch Nikon, ended his life at Dionysiou Monastery.

From there we left for the island of Corfu, to the relics of St. Spyridon, toward whom Fr. Cleopa has a great devotion.

"The next day being Sunday, we served the Holy Liturgy together, and Fr. Cleopa was invited to deliver a spiritual word at Platytera Monastery in the town. Late in the evening we went by ship to Italy to the relics of the Holy Hierarch Nicholas the Great Wonderworker, at the insistence of Fr. Cleopa, who wanted to venerate them at least once in his life and ask for the saint's help.

"At ten in the morning we arrived at Bari, where the cathedral with the relics of St. Nicholas is to be found. Here all of us worshipped with tears at his reliquary, which is kept under the altar of the big church, and we asked his help and mediation for us and for our country. Then Fr. Cleopa read with tears the first part of the Akathist to St. Nicholas, and we all sang 'Rejoice, O Nicholas Great Wonderworker!' It was a moment of great emotion which we would not forget.

"From there we departed to Rome, where we visited the Catacombs and venerated the relics of St. Callistus and St. Sebastian. Then we made a stop at Cheliye Monastery in Yugoslavia, to see the great Serbian theologian, Justin Popovich. All desired to speak with this great dogmatic theologian known throughout the world, who had been subjected to forced residence in this monastery.*

"For two days Archimandrites Justin and Cleopa conversed together through a translator. Then Fr. Cleopa asked him for personal counsel. He told Fr. Justin that he would like

---

* At the end of World War II, Rev. Dr. Justin Popovich was ousted from his post as a theological professor at the university in Belgrade, due to his influence in converting intellectuals to Christianity. He ended up at Cheliye Monastery in western Serbia, which he helped to raise up into a thriving convent, and where he served as spiritual father until his repose in 1977. He was canonized by the Serbian Orthodox Church in 2000.

Archimandrite Cleopa with St. Justin Popovich of Serbia.

to remain until the end of his life on Mt. Athos but he was in doubt. Then Archimandrite Justin said to him, 'Fr. Cleopa, if you go to the Holy Mountain, you add one more flower to the Garden of the Mother of God. But what about the faithful— to whom do you leave them? There you pray only for yourself, but in your country, you pray for all and you can bring many souls who are without guides to God. At one time I also wanted to labor in asceticism on Mt. Athos, but finally I returned to do missionary work in my country.

"'I say that you should remain in your country, and you will both save yourself and help in the salvation of others. This is the greatest good deed of monks today. Especially now, when we fight against unbelief, sects, and religious indifference.'"

"Following this counsel, Fr. Cleopa returned home in peace."

57
The Eldership of Fathers Paisius and Cleopa

In the second half of the twentieth century, Fathers Paisius and Cleopa were distinguished as the two most skilled spiritual fathers in Romania.

Both of these men gave their lives to the service of their neighbor, and each day they would receive an endless flow of visitors who came to them for spiritual nourishment and consolation. Among these visitors were their countless spiritual children, including hierarchs, monks, simple people, intellectuals, and students. Both were men of prayer gifted with the grace of tears, constant prayer, and clairvoyance. And although they both used the same spiritual method, each had his own distinctive character.

Fr. Paisius had a meek, calm, and very affectionate nature. He wouldn't refuse anyone for Confession, nor would he place any special circumstances on the penitent. He would speak slowly and sparingly, would easily forgive, and would shed tears for each one, especially for mothers, children, and the sick. Rarely did he speak of hell, but he reminded all of God's infinite mercy. He confessed day and night, receiving everyone who came to his door and reconciling all. For this reason he usually did not sleep on a bed but would doze a little in his confessional chair.*

Anytime you would call him or knock on his door, he would ask, "Who is there?" And if he was not confessing anyone, he would say, "Come on in!"

It was impossible to tell how much or at what time he ate

---

* The confessing priest in Romania sits in a chair while the person confessing kneels.

Fr. Cleopa Ilie and Fr. Paisius Olaru.

or slept. A disciple would bring him some food, setting the plate on a chair. However, he would not eat anything until he had finished the confessions of all those who were waiting.

During the rare times that he found himself free, Fr. Paisius would take his hoe and go out into the garden near his cell. Once a confessor asked him, "Fr. Paisius, why do you labor so much in the garden? Isn't it enough that you labor with the faithful?" And the Elder answered, "I come out into the air and work a little in the garden because, that way, I forget the big sins that I hear in Confession. Because the devil has the habit of constantly bringing to the mind of the confessor the sins he hears in Confession, especially bodily sins, in order to make them a temptation. So I work more alone, so that I can pray the prayer of the mind and spiritually strengthen myself. Otherwise, we cannot withstand before men, and our word and prayer have no power to change the souls of the faithful."

Fr. Paisius did not give severe penances to his spiritual children and he took into account the age, zeal, and love for Christ of each. Generally he appointed one to repeat every day Psalm 50 seven times and the "Our Father" fifteen times, to make prostrations with the Jesus Prayer, and to read the Morning and Evening Prayers, the Canon to the Savior, and the Paraclesis and Prayer to the Mother of God.

The Elder would say to the faithful who came to him for Confession, "Have patience! Do not cut yourself off from your cross!" That is, do not grumble and do not despair amid the difficulties of life. He would weep with those who wept over their sins, and he would rejoice with those who were delivered from their passions. Hieroschema-monk Paisius had the gift of clairvoyance as well. To some he would say not to depart on a journey toward evening, so as to avoid some trouble. Others he would warn not to depart from the monastery without Holy Communion; and if they obeyed him, everything would go well by his blessing. That is why not one of his disciples would depart from his word.

One time a student came to the Elder for Confession. He was in great turmoil and asked the Elder to hear his confession, despite thinking within himself that Fr. Paisius was an uneducated peasant. But when he asked the Elder to hear his confession, the Elder told him, "No, No!" The student asked him why he would not receive him, and the Elder answered, "Because I am stubborn. Go to a father who is more educated." Realizing that the Elder was reflecting back to him his own spiritual state and judgment, the student persisted, because he was in such a state of turmoil. When the young man again pleaded, the Elder refused him again, saying, "No, because my heart is of stone." Then the student broke down and began to weep within himself and the thought came to him, "I am not worthy—I do not deserve...." At this moment, Fr. Paisius led him in to his cell and confessed him. The student had written out on paper a confession of all the sins he had committed since childhood. However, inside the cell it was dark and he could not make out his writing. Then Fr. Paisius began to recount to the young man everything he had written out and more. The Confession lasted for three hours and the young man departed from the Elder as if spiritually reborn.*

Between 1973 and 1985 Hieroschema-monk Paisius was a desert-dweller at Sihla Skete, a dependency of Sihastria Monastery, near the cave of St. Theodora. Here he continued his labors as hesychast and confessor. In 1986 he fractured his leg and was brought to Sihastria and laid in bed, where he remained until the end of his life. Nevertheless, he continued to constantly confess and spiritually console monks, priests, be-

---

* This account has been recorded and added by the translator.

lievers, and even several hierarchs who would come to him for Confession.

The spiritual offspring of Hieroschema-monk Paisius, Archimandrite Cleopa, inherited many of the virtuous characteristics of his spiritual father. He had the same zeal for Christ, the same love of prayer, the same mercy toward every man who came to him, and the same almsgiving toward the poor. However, he also had his own unique spiritual qualities. Fr. Cleopa was a man very resolute and strict with himself and a great ascetic struggler. At the same time he was always cheerful and used a good-natured sense of humor to reach the heart of his listener. In his last years he would refer to himself as "Old Man Rot," humbling both himself and those who came to him. On dismissing his disciples and those who came to him for a word, he would bless them and, full of love, would say, "May Heaven consume you!"

Since he was providentially endowed with an astonishing memory and had a great love for the Holy Fathers, a living word would naturally spring forth from his mouth from the Patristic writings. He knew more Patristics and Theology than most scholars with a degree in Theology. He also knew very well the Holy Scriptures, the *Lives of Saints,* Dogmatics, Canon Law, the *Philokalia* and the whole of Patristic Literature. For this reason, he was sought out by many intellectuals and theologians. When they would ask him where he received his theological schooling he would answer with a smile on his face, "Do you see the staff behind the door? With that I would journey with the sheep. Do you see that knapsack on the nail? In it I would carry books that I had borrowed from Neamts Monastery and would read them with the sheep. Look also at the *opinci* [peasant shoes]. Do you see them? This is my science. And my schools are the hillsides where I journeyed with the sheep of the monastery for over ten years."

The eighty-six-year-old Elder with spiritual daughters and an American pilgrim. Photo taken two months before his repose.

Nevertheless, Fr. Cleopa was able to deliver lectures on these subjects at any level.

As a confessor, Fr. Cleopa was more severe than Fr. Paisius, especially with monks, priests, and theologians who had not taken the effort to make their own the Holy Scriptures and the Holy Fathers and who did not pastor the flock of Christ in the fear of God. He demanded that priests and monks lead an exemplary Christian life, so that they would be the light of the world and guides for men.

With children, mothers, the elderly, and the poor, Fr. Cleopa was very meek and merciful. No one left his cell without a small gift: an icon, a book, a little cross, a few pieces of incense, money for those without any, and the usual blessing at their departure.

A woman gives an account which exemplifies the directness of Fr. Cleopa's ministry as an elder:

"It was the end of 1995. I had been to Sihastria a few times and had met Fr. Cleopa. My father was very sick, and for almost forty years he had been tormented by the passion of drunkenness. After many attempts I came with him one day to Fr. Cleopa. He was sitting in a meadow under a tree and a few Christians were with him. We sat on the bench right in front of Fr. Cleopa, who was giving a profitable word for those who were listening.

"All of a sudden he stopped for a second and looked over our heads and began to talk about drunkenness. My father, who was sitting on the bench, became dumbfounded. This profitable word of Fr. Cleopa's lasted for a while and then he let us go, blessing each one as he normally does. I came close to him with my father, and when my father bent down, Fr. Cleopa took his head into both his hands, made a big cross, and said to him, 'So, dear one, give a complete Confession and the Mother of God will help you. May we see one another in Paradise!'

"We departed at peace. What happened then I don't know. For almost thirty years I hadn't seen my father make the sign of the Cross, but now, when we returned home, he entered the dining room and made three big prostrations. I looked at mother and she looked at me. We were astonished! Since then Father confesses regularly and has been delivered from the passion of drunkenness."

For nearly fifty-four years, as both abbot and spiritual father, Fr. Cleopa raised and formed thousands of souls for Christ—monks, laymen, priests, and hierarchs. Each one he would tell openly, in few words, what he needed to do for his salvation. For this directness he was sought out by all.

Thus, through the guidance of the two Elders, Paisius and Cleopa, Sihastria Monastery became a spiritual lighthouse through which the Romanian people were spiritually nourished in the second half of the twentieth century.

58
The Spiritual Qualities of Fr. Cleopa

1) *Prayer.* As a boy the young Constantine prayed often from books, learned many prayers by heart and continually repeated them. As a youth he developed a great love for reading the Psalter, which he repeated daily. He also knew by heart the Akathist to the Savior, the Akathist to the Mother of God, the Canon of Repentance to the Savior, and the Paraclesis to the Mother of God, which he said daily. At the same time he made three to four hundred prostrations and bows each day.

Under the influence of his ascetically minded older brothers Basil and George, he also began to force himself to become accustomed to the Prayer of the Heart, at which the older two became advanced at a young age.

As abbot of Sihastria Monastery, being very busy during the daytime hours, Fr. Cleopa would pray more at night. He slept two hours before Matins and two more hours after the service, after which he performed his entire prayer rule for the day, which took three hours. Over the course of the ten years he spent in the wilderness during his three exiles, he devoted countless hours to the Prayer of the Heart. Even the fingernail with which he pulled the knots on his prayer rope was deformed because of a lifetime of practicing this prayer.

Fr. Cleopa would speak to his disciples about pure Prayer of the Heart as if he were speaking of someone else's experience: "I met with someone who had toiled with hunger, with thirst, with cold, with nakedness in the woods, and he told me that he had once spent the night in the home of a pious Christian man. It being the evening before Sunday, he was performing his rule of prayer. At the house of a neighbor there was a wedding with music. The desert-dweller, being at prayer, had before him an icon of the Mother of God. Standing and pondering, he thought upon the word of St. John of the Ladder which says, 'Some say songs can raise the advanced to more exalted contemplations.' Thus, hearing the music from the wedding, he said to himself, 'If these people know how to sing so beautifully, how do the angels in heaven sing, who give praise to the Mother of God?' From this feeling his mind descended into his heart, and he stayed in this prayer for over two hours, feeling much sweetness and warmth. His tears flowed continually, his heart was enflamed, and he sensed Christ—how He conversed with his soul. Such a fragrance of the Holy Spirit came upon him then, and he felt so much spiritual warmth, that he said to himself, 'O Lord, I want to die at this moment!'

"After two hours his mind came out from his heart, and he remained with a sweet sorrow, a joy, a consolation, and an incredible spiritual warmth for a month. The heaven of his heart could no longer be drawn to something from this world, because the tears that stream during such times of prayer, being from the Holy Spirit, wash away all defilement and sinful imaginings, and the soul remains pure."

Fr. Cleopa would say of the Prayer of the Heart: "When the mind descends into the heart, then the heart opens up and then it closes. That is, our heart absorbs Jesus, and Jesus absorbs our heart. In that moment the Bridegroom Christ meets with the bride, that is, with our soul."

If someone asked Fr. Cleopa for a profitable word about the Prayer of the Heart, he would speak as if about someone else, so that no one would know about his activity. That is why his disciples at Sihastria did not know how much he prayed and what measure he had attained in prayer. However, the gift of tears did not abandon him until he moved on to the heavenly abodes.

Fr. Cleopa prayed for all who asked his help. If someone was tormented at the hour of death and Fr. Cleopa was called to read the prayer of departure for the soul, the dying person gave his soul peacefully into the hands of the Lord, even while the prayers of absolution were being read.

During the last twenty years of his life Fr. Cleopa spent a great deal of time at prayer: fourteen to fifteen hours a day. He had mystical moments when he did not want to speak with anyone, not even his cell attendant. He also had secret places for prayer. When he was stronger he would pray in the woods or in the mountains. In his old age he would pray more in his cell alone. Another place he preferred was the apiary of the monastery, where he had a small cell and where he kept his books and manuscripts.

Elder Cleopa at one of his favorite spots of seclusion.

His most powerful prayer was at night, standing alone in his cell, or else at the edge of the forest, since he loved nature very much—the sheep and all of God's creation. As a matter of fact, every word uttered by his holiness was a prayer and a blessing for those who asked for his help. But his interior life of prayer remained a mystery unknown to all.

2) *Fasting.* Elder Cleopa grew accustomed to fasting at a very young age. None of the Ilie children would eat dairy products on a fast day. Early on they began to keep the three-day fast at the beginning of Great Lent. Thus he was easily able to adapt to the monastic way of life at Sihastria.

At Sihastria the general practice during Great Lent was to keep the three-day fast according to the typicon. The next meal served would then be on Friday evening. Throughout the Fast one meal a day without oil was served at three in the afternoon, except on Saturday and Sunday. During Holy Week one meal a day was served toward evening, and from Thursday evening until Holy Pascha an absolute fast was observed.

The greatest faster of Sihastria was Abbot Ioanichie Moroi, who would only eat prosphora throughout the week and only on Saturdays and Sundays partake of food. Imitating his abbot, Fr. Cleopa would fast completely from Monday until Saturday during the first week of Lent, while during the other weeks he would take one meal a day toward evening.

Although Fr. Cleopa was strict with himself in fasting, he was merciful toward others who could not withstand such abstinence, especially the sick and the younger brothers. Thus he would bless them to eat two meals a day even during Great Lent.

During the time of the Great Fast Fr. Cleopa would give an example to the brothers by speaking little and would often withdraw to his hut in the nearby wilderness. He would never speak about his time in seclusion.

During his time of exile in the wilderness he would eat one potato a day and other wild plants that he found. His disciples said that, if on the last day before the Nativity Fast he had two potatoes and a beet, he would say it seemed to him like a feast day.

3) *Obedience.* Fr. Cleopa was a practitioner of obedience from his childhood until the hour of his death. Whatever command his abbot would give to him, he would scrupulously carry it out without even a trace of murmuring. Whatever word of teaching someone would give him, he would seek to carry it out with joy and humility. When any of the brothers would call for help, he would be the first to come. There was no one else who lived at Sihastria who was more obedient and more decisively ready to serve without hesitation than he was. For this he was loved more than all the other young novices during his time.

The success he enjoyed in raising up Sihastria from the ashes of the fire of 1941 into a center of spiritual enlightenment and the devoted obedience of his disciples were direct reflections of the obedience which he first exemplified as a young monk. This spiritual equity which he had gathered and the blessing of the Mother of God were the two key elements in forming the great Sihastria Monastery.

4) *The Gift of Tears.* Even as a small boy Fr. Cleopa would frequently shed tears during prayer, so much so that he would have to hide himself. In the monastery he would weep while he served the Holy Liturgy, especially at the time of the Consecration. It was in the wilderness, however, that Fr. Cleopa experienced, while performing the Prayer of the Heart,

the flooding of tears described by St. Isaac the Syrian. Even into old age Fr. Cleopa was seen by his disciples weeping when he prayed in his cell. These tears brought him much joy and consolation.

5) *Remembrance of Death.* From seeing his two brothers depart this life at such an early age, and from his experience as a youth of holding his sister in his arms while she passed away, Fr. Cleopa had the remembrance of death firmly instilled in his mind. In the period after his brothers' departure, he would often go into the cemetery and light candles on their graves and pray throughout the night. These firsthand experiences with death, together with the Lives of Saints and Martyrs who received death manfully for the love of Christ, spiritually strengthened him.

6) *Patience.* Fr. Cleopa was a man of patience and long-suffering all of his life. It was precisely through his patience, steadfastness and prayer that he succeeded in raising up so many souls for Christ and in guiding the monasteries entrusted to him.

In the face of the constant surveillance of his activity by the Securitate, he had no fear and bore no hatred toward anyone but rather had in his soul the love of Christ. He knew that without patience, without great suffering and temptations, one cannot be saved. That is why when any of the fathers would come to him in turmoil, he would recall the words of the righteous Fr. Vincent Malau, whose constant counsel to his disciples was "Listen, brother. Patience, patience, patience … and when it seems to you that you have no more and have been taken to your limit: patience, patience, patience…. Patience until the door of the grave."

7) *Stillness.* After he finished Confession, Fr. Cleopa would withdraw to stillness, especially at night, to the edge of the forest or to the cemetery, where he would pray alone. Then he would quietly say the Jesus Prayer, which had become part of his heart after so many years. Stillness would give rest to his soul and fill him with spiritual peace. And when God would visit him with the gift of tears, he would also withdraw to a secret place until God calmed down his soul.

After he had tasted of the joy of stillness in the years of his exile, Fr. Cleopa longed to remain continually in the life of solitude, since stillness is the mother of prayer, tears, and spiritual joy. But the commandment of obedience would induce him to again return to his community.

8) *Humility.* Another great gift of Fr. Cleopa was humility, which is one of the principle traits of sanctity. Father would say, "I am nicknamed 'monk,' and it happens that I call myself a monk, but I've never done anything in life. To be a true monk is a great thing. How can I say that I am a monk before men if before God I am not? A monk must be an angel in the flesh, not leading a worldly life like I do in sins and helplessness!"

Fr. Cleopa constantly humbled himself, remembering the words from Holy Scripture: *I was brought low, and He saved me* (Psalm 114:6).

"I am an empty man," Father once said. "A fruit tree with only leaves. You'd die of hunger next to it. St. Isaac the Syrian says, 'The word without works is like a man who depicts water on walls and can die of thirst next to it.' This is me. With me you'll die of hunger. I am telling you to do all this but I am not doing it myself. Why are you coming to a barren cow?"

9) *Acts of Mercy.* A fundamental virtue which characterized the whole life of Fr. Cleopa was his mercifulness toward

all. Although he was truly a non-acquisitive monk without any personal wealth, he richly distributed the gifts that the faithful brought to him. Every day widows, beggars, poor people, and mothers with big families received direct help from Fr. Cleopa—money, clothing, food, and most importantly, words of encouragement. Everyone left from a visit to the Elder thankful toward God, Who had shown such mercy through His devoted servant.

When Fr. Cleopa was abbot, he had the rule that all the faithful who had come to the monastery, no matter how many, would eat a common meal. One of his disciples from Slatina tells the story that on one feast day, when many pilgrims came, there was very little food and the monastery was in danger of running out of provisions altogether. The cook then told the Abbot, "Fr. Cleopa, if we feed everyone now, we won't have anything left to eat. What should we do?"

Then Fr. Cleopa, who never put hope in anything transitory, said, "Brother, put out everything you have! Put out everything!"

Three hours later a group of the faithful brought all kinds of food, which was enough to sustain the monastery for a good period of time.

10) *Discernment*. Crowning all the virtues that the Elder possessed was the rare gift of true spiritual discernment. To each soul that came to him, he would give counsel specifically for that individual in his particular situation.

Once a busload of people came to visit the Elder. After Fr. Cleopa had addressed the assembly for about a half an hour, each one questioned him in regard to his personal situation. Several sick people asked the Elder for advice:

"Father, I have been sick for a long time. I've gone to the doctor. What else should I do?"

"Go see a doctor and see what you have. Have an operation," the Elder said.

Another asked, "Father, I have a daughter who has been sick for a number of years at home. I have difficulties with her. What do I do? Should I take her to a doctor or not?"

The Elder replied, "Go to a doctor."

Again, another asked, "Father, I am sick. What do I do?"

"Have Holy Unction served," said the Elder to that one.

"Shouldn't I also go to the doctor?" this one persisted.

But the Elder answered definitively, "No, no! Go to the Holy Unction service!"

Thus the Elder applied to each sufferer the medicine proper to the individual. Of course he was aided in this by the grace of the Holy Spirit, through Whom he had received spiritual foresight and had become, in truth, a knower of hearts.

59
He That Endures until the End Shall Be Saved

Elder Cleopa was of a robust and vigorous character, both physically and spiritually. To his last days he retained a strong voice, with which he daily exhorted the faithful and his monks. Once he reached the age of seventy, however, his formerly strong body began to suffer. The years he had spent in the wilderness deprived of food and bodily warmth had also taken a toll on his ascetic body.

His first physical ailment was a double hernia, for which he was hospitalized in St. Spyridon Hospital in Iasi and operated on, in 1985. A few years later he was again operated on, for kidney stones, and again for a dental infection. Later he fractured his right hand. Despite all these bodily afflictions, which weakened his constitution, he still did not fall sick, and continued to function in full capacity.

In June of 1996 Fr. Cleopa underwent a fourth operation, for tumors of the bladder at the Hospital of Urology in Iasi. It was then discovered that his left kidney was inactive. Although the doctors found no more tumor lesions during his checkup of September 1996, an additional operation was proposed to him, which he refused.

Even at the hospital Fr. Cleopa's presence affected the people surrounding him. The doctors at Iasi followed a special schedule in order to hear Fr. Cleopa's spiritual talks in the hospital. Many people, hearing that the Elder was hospitalized, brought him all kinds of food. Instead of keeping the food for himself, he would call the assistants to take the food to the kitchen for the other sick people. When he checked out of the hospital, the doctors told him, "Father, as long as you were hospitalized, we didn't need to supply the hospital with any food. What you received here was sufficient for the whole hospital."

Fr. Cleopa would tell another story from that period of time: "After the operation I was brought to the intensive care unit. There I slept on a reclining chair for three days and nights. When I woke up I was told, 'Father, do you know that you slept for three days and three nights and that you talked all the time?'

"'I don't know anything! But what did I say?'

"'Father, do you know how many sermons I recorded? Look at how many I recorded!' and they showed me a whole bunch of cassettes. The sermons they recorded over those three days and nights were the sermons which I had delivered over the previous thirty to forty years."

Another story the Elder would tell about the time of his operation was the following: "When I was at Iasi for the operation, I had to have a urology exam for my kidney. It was during Great Lent. They did the exam and nothing showed up. Then a woman physician came to me and said, 'Father, in order for the urology exam to show anything, you must eat three eggs.'

"'Listen to me, ma'am. If you offered me mountains of gold, as big as the distance from Nicolina to Copou,* I wouldn't eat three eggs during the Great Fast.'

"'So that is why you've come to the hospital and that is why you'll die!'

"'And if I die, who cares? Is it the king that's dying? It's a rotten old man that's dying! So what! Am I the only one who dies? No, everybody dies.'

"'But why won't you eat eggs?'

"'Because I don't believe in eggs!'

"'What do you believe in, then?'

"'I believe in the Father, the Son, and the Holy Spirit!'

"Then she went and complained to the director of the hospital, 'There is a Father who doesn't want to eat eggs for the exam!' But the director knew me and he said to the doctor, 'Don't you know who that Father is? It is Fr. Cleopa! He spent about ten years in the wilderness and he ate one potato a day and some weeds....'

"When she heard this, she came to me in my hospital room with Lenten food that she herself had cooked, asked forgiveness, and then did the exam again.... Without any eggs.

"When they came with the X ray, they told me, 'Look at this, Father, how beautifully it came out!'

"'Ma'am, do you mean that it came out without the three eggs?'

---

* Almost three miles.

"Everybody was laughing. My left kidney was more swollen and my right kidney was normal.

"'Do you see that it came out without eggs?'

"'Father, forgive us! We've never seen such a thing since we have been practicing medicine.'"

In May of 1998, being in great pain, Fr. Cleopa agreed to go in for a checkup and stayed for one week in Iasi. However, he refused to be hospitalized, saying, "My brothers are waiting for me and I am preparing to go to them!" When another check-up was proposed in November of that same year, he again repeated the same words.

Despite all these sufferings, Fr. Cleopa's disposition remained cheerful and yet sober as he waited expectantly for the hour of death, raising his thoughts to the Crucified God and lifting his heart in ceaseless prayer.

60
In the Image of Adam

Through his many years of ascetic labor and the faithful endurance of many sufferings, Elder Cleopa had found within himself that *peace of God, which passeth all understanding* (Phil. 4:7), as the Apostle Paul says. And because of this inward peace, even nature itself responded differently to him than to other men.

One disciple remembered with fondness: "The birds would comfort Fr. Cleopa greatly. He'd often talk about the 'young braves of the forest,' the 'little owl,' and the other birds, showing us how they would sing. As he made his bird calls, our hearts were overjoyed. From the first time that he had communed at his cell in the forest, when the flock of birds came and rested on him, until his death, he had a great love for birds.

"And this love was never interrupted. Two years before the end of his life, after he had communed in church and was walking toward his cell accompanied by two other fathers, a flock of small birds came chirping pleasantly and rested on his head, on his shoulders and on his hands, and nibbled at his beard and ryassa. Yet they would not even touch the other fathers.

"As the birds flew away into a spruce tree and began to sing, Father said, 'Oh, how much I would love to live again with the birds in the woods!'"

61
His Last Days

In September of 1998, foreseeing the end of his earthly sojourn, Elder Cleopa now began to openly proclaim to his disciples, "Now I am going to my brothers!" and, "Let me depart to my brothers!" to which he would add, "I am going to Christ! Pray for me a sinner!"

At the end of September, at the setting of the sun, Fr. Cleopa asked to go to the cemetery to visit for the last time the graves of his brothers, Monk Gerasim and Ryassaphore Monk Basil, and the graves of his spiritual fathers, Hieroschemamonk Paisius and Abbot Ioanichie Moroi, together with the graves of all the fathers who had passed from this life. He visited the grave of each of his spiritual fathers, brothers, and sons, exhibiting heartfelt feeling. Supported by his disciples, he venerated the holy cross on each grave and repeated the prayer, "Pray also for Cleopa, a sinner, because, behold, tomorrow, the day after tomorrow, we will meet before Christ!"

Finally, when departing the cemetery, he uttered this prayer: "Mother of God, have mercy on us and all the fathers

Fr. Cleopa in the cemetery at Sihastria.

in this cemetery, who pray before the throne of the Most Holy Trinity in order to obtain forgiveness from the Righteous Judge."

62
Departure to Christ

Until his very last days Fr. Cleopa continued to give counsel and blessings to those who came to him. His face was serene and he spoke calmly and beautifully to those who asked him questions. He did not refuse to see anyone. He consoled all and strengthened them, as always, in stillness and joy.

On Sunday, November 29, on the eve of the feast of Romania's patron, the Apostle Andrew, the Elder was again surrounded by people. He spoke warmly, briefly, and with great meekness as the faithful went back and forth between the Elder's quarters and church.

At 11:30 A.M. a brother came to his holiness and asked for a blessing for tonsure into monasticism, saying, "Bless me, holy Father Cleopa, because this evening I will be made a monk!"

After blessing the young aspirant, the Elder placed his hand on the youth's head, and the brother asked him for a profitable word. Elder Cleopa replied, "From now on you no longer have a father, you no longer have a mother, you no longer have brothers, you no longer have relatives, you no longer have friends, you no longer have property, you no longer have a home, you no longer have anything! Only Christ!"

"Father," said the disciple, "if you obtain boldness before God, remember me in your holy prayers!"

"The mercy of the Mother of God be with us all!" replied the fading Elder.

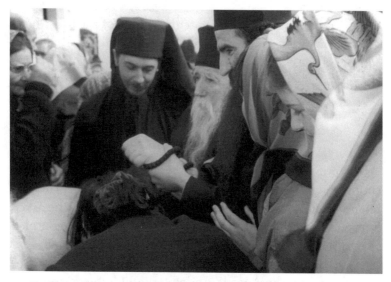

Fr. Cleopa being escorted by two of his disciples at his last patronal
feast day of Sihastria, the Nativity of the Mother of God,
September 8, 1998.

At 4:00 P.M. another brother came to ask the Elder for a
blessing for the monastic life. Fr. Cleopa did not say anything
to him but only placed his fatherly hands on the head of the
young servant of God. From this time on Elder Cleopa no
longer responded to the questions of his disciples but sat in his
confessional seat, remaining motionless with his eyes half-
open, as if in a rapture, for well over eleven hours.

On Monday morning the Elder awoke at 3:30 A.M., as if
from a deep sleep, very cheerful and spiritually contented. He
then asked for something to eat, joking, "Have you ever seen a
monk eating at this hour?"

The rest of that day and the next, the Elder stayed with
the faithful and gave counsel as usual. However, on Monday
afternoon, in an unusual way, Fr. Cleopa began to read his
Morning Prayers despite his disciples' reminding him, "Father

it's evening now. Read the morning prayers tomorrow morning!" To this the Elder answered, "I will read them now because I am going to my brothers." At this his disciples looked at him in disbelief.

On Tuesday, December 1 he went to bed late, showing signs of being very exhausted. At 2:20 A.M. on Wednesday morning, December 2, the Elder's disciple heard him begin to breathe less and less regularly. Finally, when the disciple drew close to him, Fr. Cleopa drew in one final deep breath and gave his soul into the hands of Christ.

Immediately all the fathers gathered and the tolling of the bells began. The body of the Elder was then carried in solemn procession to the old church in the monastery. The news of Fr. Cleopa's departure to the eternal dwellings quickly spread throughout the country. Thousands of the faithful, together with hierarchs, priests, and monks from all over Romania, began to arrive at the monastery to pay homage to the departed Elder.

63
Burial

For three days and nights the Psalter was read over the body of Fr. Cleopa. Continual prayer for his soul was sent up by the monks of Sihastria, by the faithful from all over the country who loved Fr. Cleopa as their father, and by many visiting hierarchs and clergy, some of whom were also the spiritual sons of Fr. Cleopa.

The burial was set for Saturday, December 5. Like a miracle, the day dawned with bright clear skies and remained sunny and warm throughout the day. This break in the weather was a true blessing, as the days that followed the burial were dark and cold.

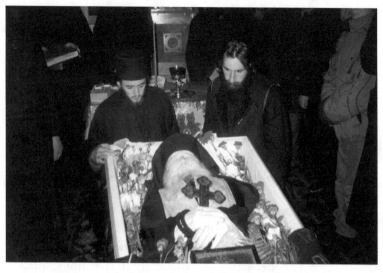

Young monks look with thoughtful gaze at their Elder
in blessed repose.

The Liturgy was served by an assembly of hierarchs composed of Metropolitan Daniel of Moldavia and Bucovina; Archbishop Bartholomew of Vadului, Feleacului and Cluj; Bishop John of Orad; Bishop Cassia of the Lower Danube; Bishop Joachim of Husi; Bishop Callinicus of Iasi; Bishop Bessarion of the Ardeal Metropolitanate; and Bishop Gerasim of Suceava and Radauti.

Following the completion of the Liturgy, the burial service was held in the monastery courtyard. The monastery enclosure was tightly packed, as over ten thousand people had turned out to pay their last respects to the spiritual father of the Romanian people. At the conclusion of the service Metropolitan Daniel gave a word on the significance of the great Elder.

Then the local shepherds blew their traditional Romanian shepherd's horns called *bucium* in tribute to the shepherd boy who had become the good shepherd of the Romanian

Death swallowed up in Victory: ten thousand people celebrate
the righteous repose of Elder Cleopa.

A shepherd with a traditional *bucium,* such as was piped at Fr. Cleopa's
funeral procession.

people. The final procession began, around the church and to
the monastery cemetery. The bells tolled and the people sang
the funeral dirge, as the body of Fr. Cleopa was brought to its
resting place alongside his beloved Elder, Paisius Olaru.

Many wept at the pain of separation from their spiritual
father and desired to touch one last time the hands which had
bestowed so many blessings during fifty years of priesthood.
Yet, in the midst of all the pain and emotion, a bright ray of
sunshine—like a ray from Heaven—shone through the thick
forest of fir trees and illuminated the freshly dug grave. As the
coffin was lowered into the sunlit grave, the more than ten
thousand believers began to sing the traditional "Memory
Eternal." But as they came to the concluding verse, the grand
assembly spontaneously and with one voice burst out singing
"Christ is Risen" as a hymn of victory.

Thus, all who had come to see Elder Cleopa one last time departed not with sorrow but rather with resounding joy, just as they had always departed from him in life.

64
The Forty-Day Memorial

On January 9, 1999, forty days after the repose of Elder Cleopa, the Holy Liturgy was served, together with the Forty-Day Memorial Service, in the winter church of Sihastria Monastery. The services were performed by Metropolitan Daniel together with a group of priests from Moldavia. Then the entire monastic community, led by Metropolitan Daniel and the Abbot of Sihastria, Archimandrite Victorin, processed to the grave of the ever-memorable Elder Cleopa and sang the Trisagion hymn, offering their final prayers for the eternal rest of the soul of their spiritual father.

According to the custom established by the Elder himself, a common meal was offered to all present—monastics, the faithful, and the poor—in commemoration of the soul of one who will forever remain in the consciousness of the Romanian people.

65
Christ is Risen!

In the spring following the repose of Elder Cleopa, a believing woman who had been close to the Elder came to the monastery for Pascha. She did not, however, stop at the Elder's cell, thinking that she had no reason to go there because he had already reposed. But that evening, while she was resting before the Paschal Service, she had a dream. She found herself in front

The path to Elder Cleopa's cell.

of Fr. Cleopa's cell, thinking that he had died. Then, all of a sudden, Fr. Cleopa appeared to her in the doorway and said to her, "Please come in. Why don't you come in?"

"But aren't you dead, Father?" she asked.

"Don't you see that I am alive?" Father said.

The next day, the Day of Resurrection, the woman went to Fr. Cleopa's cell to venerate the holy icons in the cell, believing, without a doubt, that he is indeed alive and is praying for all who ask for his help.

PART II

THE FINAL WORD
OF ELDER CLEOPA
TO THE COMMUNITY
OF SIHASTRIA

Elder Cleopa passing on teachings to his monastic brothers.

THE FINAL WORD OF ELDER CLEOPA
TO THE COMMUNITY OF SIHASTRIA
(March 1, 1998)

IN the name of the Father, and of the Son, and of the Holy Spirit!

Holy Father Abbot, Holy Fathers and Brothers, just as I see you here, beloved ones, so I will see all of you in Paradise, where joy is boundless, because all of you are in service to the Savior and to the Mother of God and each one does his obedience where he is placed. When I see you, I think of how dear you all are to me. But many of you I do not know. I come here so rarely. But I know those who come for Confession and those who are older.... I desire that all, all of you will go to eternal joy and not one, God forbid, will go to torment.

My beloved Fathers and Brothers, know that the Church is our spiritual mother. She gave birth to us at Baptism through *water and the Spirit* (John 3:5). You have heard the Apostle Paul say, *Ye have received the Spirit of adoption* (Rom. 8:15) in the font of birth, and *He saved us, by the washing of regeneration, and renewing of the Holy Spirit* (Tit. 3:5). From now on we are all sons according to the gift of God, since we were baptized in the name of the Most Holy Trinity.

That is why I ask you with all my heart to love the Mother Church. Let the Church be dear to you and, as much as is in your power, go to church day and night. Those who are elderly and can't go are allowed to spend less time there. Those who are younger can stay longer because the order of the Church enriches the memory of each one, and the grace of the

Most Holy Spirit comes over the one who listens with piety to the holy services of the Church.

My dear ones, I, a sinner and an unworthy one, am old—eighty-six years old, six operations. My right hand is broken; I was in a plaster cast for thirty-two days. Tomorrow and the day after tomorrow you will sing for me "Memory Eternal." What else am I waiting for? Psalm 89 says clearly, *As for the days of our years they be threescore years and ten. And if we be in strength mayhap fourscore years.* And the eleventh line says this, *And what is more than these is toil and travail.* I have entered into the years of pain. I have grown old; I will be eighty-six years old on April 10th.

My beloved Fathers, I ask you from my whole heart—you who have love and are able—to not forget me in prayer. To commemorate me!

I have love when I see you all in service to the Savior and the Mother of God. So I will see you in Paradise, beloved ones, all of you! All of you are serving the Savior and the Mother of God.

Our monastery is a monastery with a canonical rule: no eating of meat, regular Confession, and the services conducted according to the rule of St. Sava.

When I came here I found fourteen Fathers, wearing old peasant shoes, with beards down to their knees, with wooden prayer ropes in their hands ... my brother Basil brought me. I was seventeen and a half years old when I came here....

When I saw all the monks at the meal and the Abbot—the Elder—reading a profitable word at the head of the table from St. Theodore the Studite, I asked my brother, "Is it a feast day here?" Because I had stayed at Cozancea and there it was idiorrhythmic: each one with his own meals, his own house. "Dear brother," he said, "it isn't a feast! Here there is the common life. The monks eat together all the time!" The

Elder was reading a word to them.... He would serve the Holy Liturgy and would nourish himself only with the Holy Gifts for almost twenty years. Only on Saturday and Sunday did he taste a little something in a bowl. I know because I was the cook for a time. God give him rest. He had such a strong fear of God and such faith! He tonsured me in 1937, during the Dormition Fast. I remember.

There was a Father, Nicholas Gradinaru, with a long beard; maybe some of you know him. When I went in front of the Altar, he said, "Most Holy Father, give him the name Cleopa, because we don't have a Cleopa here!" And the Elder put his hand on the scissors and called me "Cleopa." And so it was.

God give him rest! I have a commemoration list in my cell of all those who have died here. I also have all the patriarchs and bishops. As long as I have the spark of life, I will commemorate them every day!

And I ask you, my dear ones, all of you—do not forget me in your holy prayers. Just as I see you here, I will see you in Paradise, the eternal joy without end!

The mercy of the Most Holy Trinity and the Protection of the Most Holy Mother of God and the prayers of all the saints be over you all, my dear ones, and take you all to Paradise. Amen.

Orthodox pilgrims from America visiting Fr. Cleopa in 1992.

PART III

WORDS AND DEEDS
OF INSTRUCTION

Fr. Cleopa as he looked when receiving those who came
to him for guidance.

WORDS AND DEEDS OF INSTRUCTION

1) A brother was disturbed because some children had come to the monastery and were making noise and running around on the hills. The Elder came by and the brother asked him what he should do. Fr. Cleopa said to him, "Remember, were you not a child? I love children very much because they are like angels. It is these that Christ loves and says, *Suffer the little children to come unto me, and forbid them not: for of such is the kingdom of God* (Mark 10:14)."

2) A close disciple remembered his time with the Elder: "Listening to Fr. Cleopa, you could never get your fill. Whatever he would say was interesting. He'd tell stories from his childhood, about life in the monastery, about how he was persecuted, arrested and then fled into the woods, about serving the people, about his journeys to Jerusalem and the Holy Mountain.... Often those who listened to him would weep, and sometimes Fr. Cleopa would weep. All were moved in their souls not only because of what he would say but because the grace of God worked in him. It was simply his presence, full of the grace of the Holy Spirit, that would change the hearts of men."

3) When Fr. Cleopa would speak, he would do so under the inspiration of the Holy Spirit. Once the hall next to his cell was full of people. Fr. Cleopa began to say something that seemed to have no connection with his discourse up to that point and which did not arouse much interest. But at the end a

woman who had been in the back came up to him weeping, and said to him, "Forgive me, Father, because I am a sinner!" The Elder had spoken for that woman.

4) A monk often went to the Elder, knelt, and asked for a blessing. The Elder would put his hand on his head, make the sign of the Cross, and say to him, "God bless you!" And this monk confessed that he always departed from the Elder with much peace and stillness, feeling a warmth on his head, like a fire, for more than half an hour. His soul would be filled with humility and he would shed tears.

5) Every night the Elder would go outside, especially after midnight. Even in the winter he would stay outside for at least an hour. He would pray the Jesus Prayer, listen to the night-time birds, look up into the starry sky, and rejoice in the stillness. He would go at this time when everyone was asleep in order not to be disturbed. However, the brothers would often come and disturb his quiet. Then, seeing he could not escape, he would speak to them, and after dismissing them, go back to the stillness of his cell.

6) Once, when someone showed Fr. Cleopa the new church in the monastery orchard, Father said, "It is more difficult to make a genuine monk than it is to make a cathedral!"

7) One time a believing woman from a family of intellectuals came to Fr. Cleopa distressed over the unbelief of her husband, a physics professor, who had declared himself a convinced atheist. At the suggestion of Fr. Cleopa, the woman succeeded in convincing her husband to meet the Elder, despite his claiming "I have nothing to talk about with a silly priest. No one and nothing can convince me!"

Elder Cleopa speaking on prayer to pilgrims from Western Europe,
Sihastria, summer, 1991.

When they arrived at Sihastria Fr. Cleopa was talking
with people. Although he had finished and was tired after a full
day, the Elder did not spare himself. He stayed up with the
professor, reading to him information from physics books,
talking about astronomy, about the distance between the stars,
about natural laws, about creation, and many other things.

At the end of the discussion, which lasted until midnight,
the professor took out a little notebook and asked the Elder,
"Father, in the schools where I studied I never heard such
things! How do you know so much?" And as the professor
made ready to take notes, the Elder simply replied, "And who
stops me from knowing?" At the end of their conversation the
professor asked to be confessed.

After a time his wife came back to the monastery full of
joy and told the Elder, "Fr. Cleopa, ever since my husband had

a discussion with your holiness, he has completely changed. He goes to church, he prays, and he seeks to convince others about the existence of God!"

8) One of his disciples remembered: "Fr. Cleopa constantly said things which were for the building up of the soul. An idle word was not in his mouth. He knew how to multiply his talents. In the daytime, when he didn't have pilgrims, he'd take his prayer rope and depart to the mountain. Many times I'd see him kneeling under a tree or on a tree stump, immersed in prayer. I would have to yell many times for him to hear me. If you brought him news that a group of people had arrived, at first he would be sorry for the loss of his stillness. But, being conquered by the love and the faith of those who had come, he would receive them and speak with them, strengthening them in faith and alleviating their difficulties and troubles. Then he would withdraw once again, praying that the good God would give them, 'a corner in Paradise.' He would also say, 'If I had a huge knapsack, I would put all of you in it and take you all to Paradise.'"

9) Fr. Cleopa had a great devotion to the Mother of God. He would say, "Do you know who the Mother of God is? She is the Queen of all creation, the chamber where the Word of God incarnate dwelt and through whom the Light came into the world. She is the Door of Life because Christ the Life entered into the world through her. She is the Locked Gate through which no one except the Lord has passed, as the Prophet Ezekiel said."

10) He also said, "The Mother of God is the Ladder to Heaven, the Dove that put an end to the flood of sin, just as the dove verified the cessation of the flood to Noah. She is the

Censer because she received the Divine Fire. The Mother of the Lord is the Bride of the Father, the Mother of the Word, and the Church of the Most Holy Spirit."

11) Again, he would say, "When you see the icon of the Mother of God with the Christ Child in her arms, do you know what you are seeing? Heaven and earth! Heaven is Christ, He Who is higher than the heavens, the Maker of heaven and earth. And the Mother of God represents the earth, because she is of our descent. She is from the royal and priestly lineage."

12) "Do you know who the Mother of God is and how much honor, how much power, and how much mercy she has? She is our mother because she has mercy for the poor, the widows, and all Christians. She prays continually to the Savior Christ for us all."

13) "If you want to take her as your Protectress, in the morning read the Akathist with a burning lampada, and in the evening the Paraclesis. You will have help during your life, at the moment of death, and on the Day of Judgment. Do you know what the Mother of God can do before the throne of the Most Holy Trinity? If it wasn't for her, I believe that this world would have been lost long ago."

14) To those who asked for prayers at church he would say, "I've done the big services here, but if the person doesn't do anything at home, that which is said in the Holy Scriptures is fulfilled: 'When one prays and the other does not, the one builds and the other tears down!' This is what I give you: after Morning Prayers read the Annunciation Akathist with a lamp burning. You will see that the Mother of God is a speedy helper!"

15) Fr. Cleopa constantly repeated, "Tomorrow, the day after tomorrow, I go to Christ! Tomorrow Old Man Rot departs! Tomorrow you will see me no longer—you will only see a cross in the cemetery! Memory eternal to Old Man Rot! Ah! A broken pot bound together with wire! Tomorrow I am going to my brothers. They are calling out to me, 'Come on, brother! Leave behind talking with people!'"

16) Many times when someone would sing to him, "May God grant you many years!" the Elder would stop him and say, "Not like that, but, 'Memory eternal, memory eternal, may his memory be eternal!'" or he would say, "Many years, Old Man Rot!"

17) To those who would say that they were tormented by the passion of fornication, the Elder would say, "Death, death, death! The coffin, the shovel, the spade, the pickax…. St Basil the Great says, 'When you see the most beautiful woman in the world, go with your mind to her grave a few days after she has died. Such a terrible odor and putrid flow comes from her body, such that all the latrines in the world don't smell as bad. Behold what you were lusting after!'"

18) When someone wanted to take a picture of the Elder, Fr. Cleopa would say to him, "Look for a donkey, take its picture, and write on it 'Cleopa.'"

19) A divorced man was attacked continuously by his ex-wife's relatives, who were people of great influence. The police were watching and even threatening him. He went together with his sister to ask Fr. Cleopa for his prayers. When they were ready to go, they met a monk who asked them to drive him to Sihla Skete, for he had much to carry. While they

were on the road, they told the monk of the man's troubles with the police. When they arrived at Sihla, they told the monk that the name of the policeman was Constantine. Then they departed.

The monk immediately went in front of the church and made three prostrations saying, "I thank You, O Lord, that You have brought an answer to my question as to why I have been praying for Constantine in his troubles. Now I will pray even harder for Constantine!"

As it turned out, since the policeman Constantine had been persecuting the man, his wife had fallen ill and his daughter had been in a car accident. The monk then informed Constantine that this was because of his unjust persecution of his fellow man. After that, Constantine became one of the more upright policemen on the force.

Nevertheless, the persecution of the believing man continued. His ex-wife's relatives appealed to another policeman, who threatened him, "In five days you will be in jail. The papers are ready!"

"Without any reason?" the man appealed.

"I don't need any reason, and don't forget—you will only come out of jail dead, feet first!" the angry policeman again threatened.

Hearing this, the man fled with his sister to Fr. Cleopa in the middle of the night and told him about the threat. The Elder received them but rebuked them:

"O you of little faith! Why are you afraid of people?"

"Yes, Father, but they gave us a limit—five days!"

"Leave him alone, because in three days from now, the one who threatened you will be in jail."

Indeed, after three days they found out from a judge that the policeman had been arrested. From then on the Christian man was never threatened. And when he went again to Fr.

Cleopa, the Elder told him, "Never be afraid—not just of a few policemen, nor of thousands of policemen, nor of millions, nor of billions, even if they are pointing guns at you and the bullet is ready to discharge and the finger is on the trigger. None of the guns will fire, none of the bullets will hit you if you are upright before God."

20) A believing woman left her house without her husband's permission in order to go with her mother to attend the forty-day memorial service of one of her relatives. Returning home late, she stopped along the way to see Fr. Cleopa, asking him to pray that there would be no problems with her husband when she got home. Fr. Cleopa answered calmly, "Go in peace and without fear, for when you arrive home, you will find your husband on his knees in front of the icons praying, and he won't say anything." Indeed, when she arrived home, she found her husband exactly as Fr. Cleopa had predicted.

This woman asked the Elder, "Father, how did you know what was happening?" And Father answered her briefly: "Prayer uplifts you onto the steps of knowledge. The more you pray, the better you know. And you are not afraid of anyone or anything. But pray! God and His Mother see and hear you!"

21) To those afraid of charms and spells, Fr. Cleopa would advise: "Don't be afraid of witchcraft. Have fear of God and take care not to anger Him with sin. Then spells will not have the least power! Confess your sins, fast, and go to the Holy Unction Service."*

22) When the sick would come to him, he would take their names to pray for them, and would tell them, "The great-

* The healing service of Holy Unction is performed once a week in many monasteries in Romania.

est source of healing for the sick is the Holy Unction Service. But do not have it served if the person has not confessed. First of all one should confess all one's sins, and only then have the Holy Unction Service served, with at least three priests."

23) When someone was worried about present times and would ask him, "What will happen, Father?" the Elder would answer, "The years and times the Father has placed in His dominion. As the Father wills, so will He do!" And if someone would say, "The weather outside is bad," Father would respond, "All that the Lord gives is good!"

24) To monks and brothers who wanted to go into the wilderness, he would say, "Have you had twenty years in the monastery, working at the lowest obediences? Only then can you go into the wilderness! 'Whoever wants to go into the wilderness,' St. Basil the Great says, 'have him take one or two others together with him; and he must have the experience of obedience and of the cutting off of his own will in the monastery.'"

25) Fr. Cleopa would say, "A spiritual father for nuns is to be at least fifty years old and to have had twenty years of obedience in a monastery."

26) About the Church he would say, "The Church is our Mother. Do not leave the Church, for here we are united with Christ. Here Martha and Mary are reconciled."

27) When asked by the faithful whether it was good to read the Psalter, Fr. Cleopa would say, "St. Basil the Great says that 'it is better for the sun to stop its journey than for the Psalter to remain unread in the homes of Christians.' Let us ap-

proach the Psalter like we eat a good cake. When you are hungry, you cut another piece and eat a little more; likewise, do a little more work and then read another kathisma, or two or three, as many as you can."

28) "Fr. Cleopa," a disciple said, "tell us how it was during those ten years in the wilderness. What kind of temptations did you have? I heard that you fought with the enemy! How and with what were you tempted?" The Elder replied, "If you want to know how the wilderness is, go and stay for one year and you will see."

29) The most frequent counsel he would give to monks was this: "If you want to go straight before God, you need two walls. Not of brick or stone or earth, but two spiritual walls. Have fear of God on the right, because the prophet Daniel says, 'With the fear of God man is diverted from evil.' On the left have fear of death, because the son of Sirach says, 'Son, remember your end and you will not sin.' These two good deeds—fear of God and remembrance of death—deliver a man from all sin."

30) Another brother said to the Elder, "Father, pray for me, a sinner, and if you go to the Lord, don't forget me."
"Yes, you eat and sleep to satiety and you want me to pray for you!?" the Elder rebuked him, teaching him to take responsibility for his spiritual life.

31) A Father asked the Elder how to pray and the Elder said to him, "First pray with your mouth, because from the mouth the prayer passes to the mind and then to the heart. And for this we need much labor, many tears, and the grace of the Holy Spirit."

32) To one brother he said, "Be prepared to suffer, to take beatings, to be hungry and thirsty. And if they kick you out, do not depart! Stay at the entrance of the monastery, and if the police take you away, come back and die in the monastery!"

33) One brother asked the Elder, "Father, if we are imprisoned for our faith and our mind is altered through hypnosis, do we have any guilt?"

The Elder told him, "It isn't possible to change anyone if he has in his heart the Jesus Prayer.... But you must be already practicing a life of prayer. When you say, 'Lord Jesus ...' all of hell trembles, if only you say it from the heart."

34) "How many clothes should a monk have?" someone asked him. "Two sets of clothes! Why? Do you want to become a desert-dweller with a cartload of clothes? And when they tear, put on a yellow patch, a red one, a green one!..."

35) To those who were more lazy, Father would say, "Put the carcass, that is, the body, to work, and the mind at the feet of the Lord, that is, to prayer...."

36) A brother asked Fr. Cleopa how he could be saved. Fr. Cleopa answered, "Patience, patience, patience...."

The brother asked, "What must I bear patiently?" and Father said, "Bear patiently all insults and dishonor for the love of Christ!"

37) Once a brother came to Fr. Cleopa after listening to him many times and asked him, "Father, what should I do to save myself?" And Father, who knew his heart, gave a response according to measure: "Do what you know and you will save yourself!" Then the brother realized that he already knew this

and that the only thing he was lacking was putting into practice the words of the Holy Fathers about spiritual life.

38) About endurance the Elder once said, "When you have stayed in the monastery for nine years and have taken seven beatings a day and food once every three days, then you will be a good monk!"

39) Once a brother boasted of how he desired to suffer for the Lord. Seeing that there was pride in his boldness, the Elder said to him, "I want to see what you will do when you are taken away in a car by the Securitate!"

40) A Christian said to the Elder, "Father, I do not believe that the devil exists!" The Elder, after he had taught him sufficiently from the Holy Scriptures, said to him, "If you still don't believe that the devil exists, go into the wilderness, dare to fast and pray, and he won't leave you alone."

41) Again, he said to the brothers, "Everything is transitory! Have care for the soul, confess, partake of Holy Communion, lead a pure life, give alms of mercy, do all that you can, and live in love with one another, because love never dies."

42) On prayer the Elder would say, "Prayer is the nourishment and life of the soul. Just as the body dies without food and drink, so also the soul dies without prayer."

43) He would also say, "Have the heart of a son toward God, the mind of a judge toward yourself, and toward your neighbor, the heart of a mother."

44) The Elders of Sihastria would tell of the following

miracle which they witnessed at the reliquary of St. Paraskeva on October 14, 1951: On the feast day, when people were waiting to venerate, two elderly women were waiting in line. Seeing so many people in front of them, they asked Fr. Cleopa, "Father, grant us permission to venerate St. Paraskeva without having to wait in line, because we are sick. We only want to put underneath her head this pillow which we brought from home in gratitude for the help she has given us!"

"God bless you," Fr. Cleopa said. "Go and venerate."

When the two women approached the body of St. Paraskeva, a thing altogether miraculous occurred: St. Paraskeva raised her head by herself, and after the women had placed the pillow under her head and had venerated the Saint, St. Paraskeva laid her head back down on the pillow.

45) A disciple asked the Elder, "What is pure prayer?"

"To speak it with the mouth, to understand it with the mind, and to feel it with the heart," the Elder replied.

46) Again he would say, "Obedience without prayer is servitude, but he who does obedience with prayer performs Liturgy."

47) He would also say, "Humility is born from obedience without grumbling."

48) Again: "Prayer is not conditional on time or place. It is nourishment of the soul."

49) Fr. Cleopa would say, "Never give counsel to anyone as long as you don't live it. He who gives counsel and does not live it is like a spring of water painted on a wall. But he who speaks from his experience is like a living spring."

50) The Elder would say to his disciples, "My boy, don't stand around to no purpose and lose time. Take a book in your bag wherever you go, with the sheep or with the cows or wherever you are sent, and read the word of God!"

51) He also said, "If I read a book two or three times, I almost know it by heart."

52) Sometimes he would tell us, "The Holy Fathers stop me from speaking more, for they say, 'Don't tell your own stories.' But I will tell you this much—if you had been in the wilderness and had been tied to a tree and had seen a demon, you would have uprooted that tree from the ground and run with it on your back!"

53) He also said that, around the year 2000, divine signs would be shown; and he cited St. Agathangel who had prophesied this.

54) A disciple of the Elder told us, "Many letters would come to Fr. Cleopa with all sorts of troubles and problems, and his holiness would tell me to answer them. Many Christians would also come, and Fr. Cleopa would have me speak to them and write down their names for commemoration. Thus I, being very busy, would not succeed in doing all of my monastic prayer rule, and I asked him what I should do. He said to me, 'Do your obedience, write the letters, talk to the people, and say the Jesus Prayer—for "the benefiting of your brother is your fruit," as the Holy Fathers say.'"

55) In 1996, when the head of the Holy Apostle Andrew was brought to Iasi, a brother wanted to go and venerate. A driver offered to take him to Iasi. But the brother wanted to go

without the Abbot knowing, so he went to receive a blessing from the Elder, as he was also his spiritual son.

The Elder, when he saw the brother coming for a blessing, said with a loud voice, "My, my.... Brother, you have an abbot and a God!"

"What should I do? Go to the Abbot and ask him?" asked the disciple.

"Yes, go and ask for a blessing." Fr. Cleopa answered.

56) During Confession, the Elder would act in the following way. If the penitent was a lover of praise, the Elder would defame himself, saying that he was more sinful, more avaricious, and more evil than anyone, thereby revealing the disciple's weakness.

57) He also shunned the praise of men. Once a reporter came to do an interview with him and said, "The people want light, they want living water...."

"Yes! The people have light from the Holy Gospel, from the Prophets, from the Apostles, from the Holy Fathers, from the great hesychastic saints, and from the millions of martyrs.... Therefore they have a source of light!"

"Only darkness can come from someone like me. Because I am the son of darkness, not the light. I am a sinful man, full of wickedness, full of weakness and sleepy.... I do not have love of God, I do not have self-restraint, I do not have discernment, I do not have anything! Everything, everything I've lost through my laziness, and I don't have anything good in this world!

"The Apostle Paul says thus in the First Epistle to Timothy: *Christ Jesus came to save sinners, of whom I am chief.* If that one who was raised up to the Third Heaven says that he is the chief of sinners, what can I say? That I've done good? Never, unto ages of ages."

58) A brother asked Fr. Cleopa to commemorate him in prayer. Tracing with his hand an imaginary trail winding along on the ground, the Elder said to him, "My prayer is like the smoke of Cain! It just drags on the ground...."

59) The Elder often quoted the Savior's words, *Woe unto you, when all men shall speak well of you!* (Luke 6:26), and added, "Or when your praise will surpass your deeds!"

60) When people would come troubled that antichrist was deceiving the people, that there would be wars and other such things, Fr. Cleopa would say with a strong voice, "The Father is at the helm!" and he would read verse 10 from Psalm 32: *The Lord scattereth the plans of the heathens, He setteth aside the devices of the peoples, and He bringeth to nought the plans of princes.*

Then he would strengthen them: "Do not be troubled and do not be afraid, because it will not be how they want it to be. Oh, how much they would like to do something! But don't be afraid. Pray and make the sign of the Cross with faith, and all the demons will flee!"

61) Fr. Cleopa would also say: "Do not do anything without signing yourself with the the sign of the Cross! When you depart on a journey, when you begin your work, when you go to study, when you are alone, and when you are with other people, seal yourself with the holy Cross on your forehead, your body, your chest, your heart, your lips, your eyes, your ears. All of you should be sealed with the sign of Christ's victory over hell. Then you will no longer be afraid of charms or evil spirits or sorcery, because these are dissolved by the power of the Cross like wax before fire and like dust before the wind."

62) Once a woman came to Fr. Cleopa with her grandson who was accused of a crime but was not guilty. The grandson told Fr. Cleopa that he was being tried by the law for murder, but he did not tell him that he was innocent. Fr. Cleopa stopped him and said, "You are not guilty and you will not have to go to prison!" Indeed, the youth was delivered from this unrighteous accusation.

63) While the Elder was in reclusion at the apiaries of the monastery, a believer came to him, crying because he was being sought by the Securitate. After he told the Elder the situation and gave him his name so that Fr. Cleopa could pray for him, the Elder said to him, "From now on, no longer be afraid!" Indeed, from then on he was no longer pursued.

64) A young man who had come to the monastery with the thought of staying only two or three months went to confession to Fr. Cleopa. The Elder said to him in an innocent and determined voice, "You came to Old Man Costachi. Don't leave from here." And so it was, for by the mercy of God he remained in the monastery.

65) A brother had begun some ascetic struggles greater than his strength. He was not sleeping in a bed, he read the Psalter often, and he made many prostrations, but not with a proper purpose. He was seeking only the calming of the fleshly passions, without cutting off the passions of the soul. That is why he was angry, he would judge, he would condemn, and he would have temptations.

Then he went to Fr. Cleopa in order to ask his blessing. The Elder showed him a saying that was written on the wall below an icon and said, "Take a look and see what is written there: 'The good is not good when it isn't done wisely.' I wrote that there."

66) In general Fr. Cleopa was not in favor of exaggerated ascetic labor, even though he himself had struggled greatly in the wilderness. But saints are always strict with themselves and full of love for others.

He would say that the forest is not afraid of him who takes a great deal of wood at once and overloads the cart, because it knows that the cart will break down. The forest is afraid of him who takes a small load, because, bit by bit, he will clear the forest.

67) A monk would tell the story of how he ended up at the monastery: "Coming to the monastery and listening to Fr. Cleopa, I thought to myself that I too would take on the yoke of Christ. But I was undecided. Then I thought that I would ask the Elder, because he was the one who inspired in me zeal for Christ. I said to myself, 'Whatever he says to me, that I will do!'

"When I asked Fr. Cleopa, he said to me, as if knowing my heart, 'Do not come! Stay in the world and do missionary work!' Then I became more zealous and distributed holy books.

"After about two years, when my heart inclined completely toward monasticism, I decided to go the monastery, but with a certain fear, thinking upon the word of the Elder. Praying to God, I came to him and said, 'Father, I want to come to the monastery.'

"'Come!' the Elder said, filling me with joy."

68) Once an abbot came from a monastery to Fr. Cleopa for counsel. He said that his monks did not have enough time for prayer because of the immense amount of work that needed to be done. Determined to fulfill the Elder's advice, he asked, "What should I do, Fr. Cleopa? Should I limit the ac-

tivities and work?" Fr. Cleopa answered him, "Keep to the royal path! That is, without extremes, not one way or the other. But do everything with discernment."

69) Two young people were married and had children. However, they discovered that they were blood relatives. Their spiritual father advised them to confess to a hierarch and to follow his counsel. In time the husband was told to also ask for the counsel of Elder Cleopa Ilie, whom he had never met.

Going to the Elder, he was not able to approach him, since the Elder was surrounded by a great crowd. As he waited for his turn, all of a sudden he heard the Elder call out, "Anthony, come to me!" He thought the Elder was calling another Anthony in the crowd and he did not come forward. After a time he heard again, "Anthony, come to me!" But, not realizing that the Elder was calling him, he still did not come. Finally Fr. Cleopa looked straight at him, motioned for him to come, and said, "You, the one there, Anthony, come to me!"

Seized with fear, Anthony said to himself, "How does this Father, who has never seen me before, know my name?" The Elder then talked with him for a long time. The young man left with a peaceful spirit and with the weight of his fears lifted.

70) Two women haunted by the devil came to Fr. Cleopa, who blessed them and said, "After three Holy Unction services you will be healed." And so it came to pass by the will of God.

71) A brother, seeing Fr. Cleopa sitting on the porch, drew close to him, kissed his hand, and asked for his blessing. However, he would not open his heart to the Elder because bad thoughts were warring with him in his heart. Looking at his face, Fr. Cleopa said to him, "Brother, go to your confessor,

confess yourself totally, and ask for a penance in order to free yourself from these unclean thoughts which master you."

72) When he spoke to the people, Fr. Cleopa often said, "The angels of God have brought you to the holy monasteries, dear ones. You do not see them, but each of you has next to him a guardian angel." And the Elder would look meekly at the people, as if he could see their angels.

73) To some of the fathers he would say, "It is not possible to pull anyone out of hell except by the mercy of God and good deeds."

74) Once a believer came to see Fr. Cleopa with a relative of his who was attracted to the Jehovah's Witness sect. Through many discussions and arguments, the believer had tried to bring his relative back to the right faith, but he could not convince him to abandon the Jehovah's Witnesses. Finally he convinced him to come and talk with Elder Cleopa.

As usual there were many people at the Elder's cell. They were listening to Fr. Cleopa deliver a sermon on the theme of "How the Devil Deceives Man." The believer waited in anticipation for Fr. Cleopa to finish the sermon, so that he could instigate a discussion between the Elder and his relative.

At that moment, however, he saw that his relative's face was completely transformed. His countenance was now very cheerful, radiating an indescribable joy. Listening to the sermon of Fr. Cleopa, his heart was profoundly moved, so that he no longer wanted to debate anything. And when the believer wanted to open the discussion with Fr. Cleopa, his relative said, "I no longer have anything to ask! I have never seen such a man in my life!"

This was one of the numerous cases in which simply the

presence of Elder Cleopa was sufficient to change a person's heart.

75) After only a few months in the monastery, a novice came to the Elder and said, "Father, I have a big grudge against the demons. Grant me permission to read the exorcism of St. Basil the Great!" Fr. Cleopa said to him, "You? O my goodness! You have a grudge against the demons? May you see what a grudge they have against you!... Be sure never to do such a thing.... Do you hear? He came just the other day into the monastery and now he wants to curse the devil and read the exorcism of St. Basil the Great! A great hero!"

Thus the Elder humbled the spiritual pride of the novice.

76) Fr. Cleopa would say, "Let us have the conviction that every moment we anger God. Without this humility from the heart, we cannot be saved."

77) Fr. Cleopa often reminded us of the multitude of sins that come from the wellspring of love for oneself. He would urge all to repentance, saying, "The spring of all wickedness and of all sin is love for oneself! Love for oneself is the irrational love for the body, and it is the most difficult and most subtle of all the passions that enslave human nature.

"From love of oneself are born self-pity, the sparing of oneself, self-justification, praise of oneself, self-content, self-opinion, and all the other sins, known and unknown."

78) A monk asked Fr. Cleopa, "We are often tired from our obediences and are not able to pray. What do we do?"

The Elder answered, "Brother, the body is Martha and the soul is Mary. Martha labors for those things which are earthly, while Mary, who represents the soul, stays at the feet of the Lord and prays. That is why the Lord says that *Mary hath chosen that good part* (Luke 10:42). We are obliged to reconcile Martha and Mary, that is, first of all we pray, and then we do our obedience, with the prayer of the mind and heart."

79) To women who said they had bad husbands, Fr. Cleopa said not to divorce, but rather to pray for their husbands. "These are not my words but the words of the Holy Apostle Paul: *For what knowest thou, O wife, whether thou shalt save thy husband?... The unbelieving husband is sanctified by the [believing] wife,* and vice versa" (1 Cor. 7: 16, 14).

To men he gave the same advice. And many rejoiced, seeing miracles in their homes.

80) Fr. Cleopa told us: "When I was a brother in Sihastria Monastery, no one would lock his cell because no one had anything to steal. We had everything we needed given to us from the community. But see how the enemy of our salvation wanted to seize me with the love of money! In 1937, when I was the monastery cook, a pilgrim said to me, 'Look, Fr. Cleopa, what a beautiful new coin was minted,' and he gave me one. I took the coin to my cell and put it on the windowsill under a piece of paper so that no one could see it, and I locked the door. While I worked in the kitchen, I was constantly running to my cell to make sure the coin was there. One day I realized that the enemy had attached my heart to money, because I was locking the door of my cell and always thinking about the coin. Therefore I made the sign of the Cross, unlocked the door of my cell, and gave the coin to a pauper. Thus I was delivered from the love of money!"

81) When Fr. Cleopa had a terrible temptation of fornication in the wilderness, he was shown the demon of bodily se-

duction. The demon said to him, "Won't you fall into fornication now?" Fr. Cleopa replied, "Anyone can fall, for what is man and what is woman?—they are decomposition and stench."

Another time, when he had a similar temptation, he put his feet onto live hot coals in order to drive away the demon of fornication.

82) When Fr. Cleopa would speak and give counsel, he would constantly refer to the Elders he had known, saying, "Fr. Ioanichie Moroi would say ..."; "Fr. Paisius Olaru would say ..."; "Fr. Vincent Malau would say ..." For the Elders who loved Christ possessed great spiritual wisdom.

83) Fr. Barsanuphius was tonsured a monk in 1952 and was ordained a deacon and priest in 1956 in Sihastria Monastery. He was one of the most faithful disciples of Fr. Cleopa. In 1997, when it was time for Fr. Barsanuphius to go to the Lord, Fr. Cleopa read the prayers for the departure of the soul. When he said, "Absolve Thy servant Priest Barsanuphius from pain and bitterness, and give him rest where the righteous repose," Fr. Barsanuphius breathed two times and gave his soul into the hands of the Lord. Fr. Cleopa continued praying, "For thou art the rest of our souls and bodies, and to Thee we give glory...."

84) During Fr. Cleopa's early days as a novice in the sheepfold, his sister Catherine would sometimes come and visit him. Seeing him always with the sheep, she would say, "Dear brother, are you forever to be with the sheep? At home with the sheep—here with the sheep!" But the obedient Br. Constantine would answer, "Go away from me with that kind of talk!"

85) To those preparing for the priesthood Fr. Cleopa would say, "You can always give the penance of almsgiving, except to those who are rich, because they have pockets overflowing with money. They come, put a heap of money on the table, and say, 'That's it! I've saved myself!' But the Kingdom of Heaven is not purchased with money!

"Have them fast, make prostrations, keep vigil … because then they labor and they have a reward from God. [The penance of] almsgiving can be given to one who is poorer and has to labor for money, and who thereby has a reward from God."

86) From 1930 to 1934 there lived in the Neamts region a church chanter named Nicholas Dumitru. He was a very pious believer and would come to Sihastria. When he sang at the cliros many tears were shed and many souls were brought to contrition.

Then he became sick and died. While they were carrying him to the cemetery, he awoke from the dead and lived a few more years. With tears he would always tell the story of how he had seen the torments of hell and those who were burning in that fire. And when he would sing at the cliros all the people would weep. Once someone asked him, "Why do people cry when you sing?"

He answered, "When you sing from the heart, it reaches the heart."

While Fr. Cleopa was young and just a newcomer to the monastery, the chanter Nicholas said to the older brothers, "Do you laugh at him? … know that he will be abbot!"

This prophecy was fulfilled in 1945.

87) During his longest stay in the wilderness Fr. Cleopa was accompanied for much of the time by a cell-attendant, Fr.

Barsanuphius. The story of Fr. Barsanuphius' entrance into the monastery is an interesting one:

He was married and worked in the woods. One day his log tool was stolen, and he came to Sihastria to ask for prayers for the discovery of the thief. Then Fr. Cleopa spoke a few spiritual words which made him forget about his tool and ponder whether it was possible for him to enter the monastic life.

After he had confessed to his spiritual father and had read more holy books, he decided to live in chastity with his wife. Then he began to have major temptations to relinquish the idea of serving Christ in the monastic state. One night the evil one came to them in the form of an ugly, blackened, and beardless man and roared so loudly that the house shook and the windows cracked. The enemy said to them, "Wretched ones, what are you doing to me?" Then he disappeared. After three days they both departed for the monastery, the husband to Sihastria and the wife to Old Agapia.

88) In the last years of his life Fr. Cleopa had moments of great weariness, such that he could no longer receive anyone. He would say to his disciple, "Lock the door twice, and even if the Emperor of Japan comes, do not disturb me." But if he would not be awakened for the Emperor of Japan, for the love of Christ the King and the faithful he would always rise when he was called, and he would console them, teaching and blessing them all.

89) Beginning in 1996, for two years Fr. Cleopa endured great pain from his right kidney, which was not functioning. From the onset of his illness he did not want to go to the doctor, nor did he want to take medicine. He would only take a little tea at a meal, for he had a saying: "The best food is tea with bread. Light food!" Then with great difficulty he went to

the doctor as an obedience to His Beatitude Metropolitan Daniel and the Father Abbot. And only with great reluctance did he agree to take pills and injections.

90) Elder Cleopa possessed spiritual sight. From the whole multitude of people who came to him, he knew those who performed good deeds. He would not say anything, but would look at them in a special way and bless them.

91) Once an ascetic brother came to Fr. Cleopa, saying, "Father, bless me to eat once a day, after sunset." "You, brother," the Elder said, "don't you see how weak in constitution you are? You are to eat twice a day—may Heaven consume you!"

92) At times the Elder would say, "Teach yourself how to fast, because the time will come when you will eat one potato a week!"

93) A disciple asked the Elder what would happen after he departed to the Lord. Fr. Cleopa answered, "There will be strong cold spells and difficult frosts."

94) Shortly before the Elder departed to the Lord, two Christian women came to him for his blessing and a profitable word. He told them, "I am going now to the Lord, but difficult times are coming!"

95) Fr. Cleopa foresaw his end and would speak about it in parables. Once he said, "I can see a big and beautiful cross at the head of my grave." Before it was engraved, Fr. Cleopa would repeat exactly what was later written on his epitaph.

96) One of his disciples said in simplicity about Fr.

Cleopa, "There is much to be said about our holy Fr. Cleopa. But the greatest thing about him is that his holiness had God in his heart. He was fully alive in God and God was fully present in him."

97) Before the Elder's death, a brother found in the orchard of the monastery an apple tree that had fruit with a special taste. That is why he called them "apples from the Garden of Paradise." He wanted to bring some to Fr. Cleopa but he was too timid. But Father, knowing his thoughts, told him, "Go and bring them to me now because next year you will not be able to bring them."

98) Being very weak and tired in the evening of December 1, 1998, Fr. Cleopa said to a priest to whom he was very close, " Fr. Michael, this is my final word: Watch and pray, because you do not know the day or the hour when the Son of Man will come!" Then he said, "Pray also for me. Pray!"

99) A disciple remembers the last days of Elder Cleopa: "Thursday and Friday nights, just a few nights before he went to the Lord, I slept in the Elder's cell. I marveled at his asceticism. He didn't sleep at all. He was striving to read the prayers but couldn't because he was very tired and helpless. He was praying with the mind, with his hand on the prayer rope, and he could not keep his eyes open in order to read the prayers. He would lie down for a little and then get up again and continue laboring in prayer."

100) A woman from Constanta came to Sihastria a month before the Elder departed to the Lord. She was very close to him. Later she told us the following: "I came to Fr. Cleopa's cell on October 29, 1998, to ask for a profitable word.

He told me, 'Sister, when you come again to Sihastria, you will go up there to the cross in the cemetery and tell me everything that you have to say and, if God allows, I will hear you and I will help you.'"

101) The cell-attendant of the Elder acknowledged after his repose: "Many people, remembering Fr. Cleopa, obtained courage and zeal in order to go on the path of the Lord. Peace, joy, and the spirit of holiness were felt by those who entered into the Elder's cell, even lay people. This was felt even when his cell was empty, without even an icon and without anything. Not long ago Father was imparting words, and now he imparts spirit into the hearts of the faithful."

102) A disciple of Elder Cleopa, Monk Hyacinth, testified the following: "I believe that Fr. Cleopa was one who saw events in advance in the Spirit. He told me many things when he was alive and I would not believe them, but they were fulfilled just as the Elder had said. I believe that Father saw my heart and told me what is most beneficial to me. Then I did not understand him. It would have been better if I had been obedient with heedfulness and faith. Nevertheless, he loved me and gave me what was most beneficial for my salvation. I believe that Fr. Cleopa is a saint! I feel his help. I feel he is with me! The remembrance of the Elder gives me peace, stillness, joy, and hope, because he prays for me."

103) Fr. Ioanichie Balan, a close disciple of Elder Cleopa, tells of the growing veneration of the righteous Elder: "Many of the faithful are writing to us after Fr. Cleopa's departure to the Lord and are telling us that they feel the help of his prayers. One woman gave testimony that a relative of hers, being very sick, fell into a state of despondency. In her grief she cried out,

Elder Cleopa with the living confessor Fr. George Calciu and the
spiritual writer Archimandrite Ioanichie Balan.

'Fr. Cleopa, help me!' She was seized with such joy and peace
that she no longer desired either health or anything else, and
now she is joyfully carrying her cross."

*   *   *

Many people venerate the cell and the grave of Fr. Cleopa
and take earth as a blessing. They testify to the closeness of the
Elder's presence and the power of his prayers. Reflecting on all
the testimonies written in this book and many others which
are not written, we are sure that the good God will settle him
together with the hosts of the monastic Holy Fathers. For this,
we dare to pray at his cell and his grave, saying,

"Holy Father Cleopa, if you have acquired grace and
mercy before Christ God, pray also for us, your sinful children!"

SLAVA DOMNULUI!

Portait of Elder Cleopa, painted after his repose.

Glossary

Akathist: a special service to Jesus Christ, the Mother of God, or a saint, during which one should stand; literally, "not sitting."

All-night Vigil: a service sung on the eve of a special feast; it is usually comprised of Vespers, Matins, and the First Hour.

Altar: the part of an Orthodox church behind the iconostasis, where the preparation and consecration of the Body and Blood of Christ take place.

Ambo: a raised platform in front of the Royal Doors of the iconostasis in an Orthodox church.

Antimension: a cloth representing the Savior's shroud in which His Body was lain. This cloth contains a piece of relic, and upon this the Divine Liturgy is celebrated.

Archimandrite: the highest rank conferred upon a priest-monk.

Axion Estin: a hymn to the Mother of God beginning with the words "It is truly meet." Sometimes referred to simply as *Axion.*

Canon: a set of hymns and verses sung to a particular saint or in honor of a feast. Also, a rule or decree of an historic church council.

Cell: the room or dwelling place of a monastic.

Cliros: the place in church where the services are read and sung.

Coenobium: a monastery in which monastics live a common life under an abbot or abbess.

Ecclesiarch: in a monastery, one who is responsible for the good order of the church and the service books.

Exonarthex: in some churches, the outer portico.

Hermitage: a monastic dwelling, traditionally of a solitary monastic—but often this word is used interchangeably with the word "monastery."

Hesychast: a person who lives in a state of stillness and concentration, typically devoting most of his time to the practice of the Jesus Prayer.

Hierodeacon: a monk who is in the rank of deacon.

Hieromonk: a monk in priestly rank.

Hieroschema-monk: a schema-monk in priestly rank.

Holy Gifts: the Body and Blood of Christ consecrated during the Divine Liturgy

Horologion: literally, the "Book of Hours," containing the daily cycle of services.

Hours: daily prayer services which include readings from the Psalms. Originally performed in the early Church at regular intervals according to the Roman clock.

Iconostasis: an icon-screen partitioning the altar area from the nave of the church. The Royal Doors (also called Holy Doors) and deacons' doors allow the clergy and acolytes to enter or exit the altar.

Jesus Prayer: a short prayer of supplication to Christ, "Lord Jesus Christ, Son of God, have mercy on me, a sinner," or, in shortened form, "Lord Jesus Christ, have mercy on me." See also *Prayer of the Heart.*

Kamilavka: head covering (without veil) worn by monks.

Kathisma: a division of the Psalter.

Kellion: A small monastic dwelling.

Kontakion (pl. *kontakia*): a hymn used in the Divine services in honor of a particular saint or feast.

Lampada: an oil lamp, usually hanging before an icon.

Lavra: a large coenobitic monastery.

Matins: one of the daily services which takes place late at night or early in the morning. (According to the daily cycle it is scheduled at 3:00 A.M.) This service is comprised chiefly of Psalms and a Canon of hymns which differ from day to day.

Moleben: a prayer service in which the faithful ask for heavenly help or give thanks to God.

Obedience: in addition to its ordinary meaning, it signifies a duty assigned and carried out as part of one's obedience to the superior or elder.

Pannikhida: a service of prayer for those who have reposed.

Paraclesis: a supplicatory service to the Mother of God, including the Canon to her.

Pascha: the Feast of the Resurrection of our Lord Jesus Christ.

Philokalia: an anthology of classic ascetical writings compiled by St. Nikodimos of the Holy Mountain and St. Makarios of Corinth, inspired by and based upon the previous Patristic labors of St. Paisius Velichkovsky.

Prayer rope: a knotted rope commonly used by monastics and many Orthodox Christians in saying the Jesus Prayer.

Prayer of the Heart: prayer—particularly the Jesus Prayer—that is carried on noetically in the heart, sometimes of its own accord.

Proskomedia: service of preparation for the Divine Liturgy.

Prosphoron (pl. *prosphora):* a small round loaf of bread prepared especially for the Divine Liturgy.

Protosingul: An honorary rank bestowed upon priests.

Relics: the body or pieces of bone of a saint, or objects associated with a saint or holy person, which are venerated by the faithful.

Ryassa: the outer cassock worn by tonsured monastics.

Ryassaphore: a monastic who wears a ryassa but has yet to be fully tonsured a monk or nun.

Schema-monk, schema-nun: one who has taken on the highest and strictest monastic discipline, leading a life of seclusion and prayer. He or she wears the "schema," a special cowl and stole.

Semantron: a wooden board which is struck with a mallet to call the faithful to church.

Six Psalms: Psalms 3, 37, 62, 87, 102 and 142, intoned by a reader in the center of the church at the beginning of Matins.

Skete: a small monastery; usually a close-knit "family" with an abbot or abbess as its head.

Synaxis: a gathering, host or multitude, such as a gathering of saints.

Theotokos: the Greek word for the Mother of God; literally, "God-birthgiver."

Tonsure: the rite whereby a novice is clothed in the monastic habit and becomes a monk or nun.

Trapeza: the monastery refectory; also the communal meal in the refectory.

Trisagion: the Church hymn "Holy God, Holy Mighty, Holy Immortal, have mercy on us," followed by other prayers.

Troparion (pl. *troparia):* a hymn used in the daily cycle of services and also at Divine Liturgy in honor of a particular saint or feast.

Typicon: the order of Divine services. Also, the rules and ordinances of a particular monastery.

Vespers: the daily evening service which begins the liturgical day. It consists of Psalms, hymns and verses composed in honor of the feast or saint commemorated on a particular day.

Unction: the sacrament of anointing the sick or dying.

INDEX

Page numbers for illustrations are in boldface italics.

St. Herman Press

ST. HERMAN OF ALASKA BROTHERHOOD

For over three decades, the St. Herman Brotherhood has been publishing works of traditional spirituality.

Write for our free 96-page catalogue, featuring sixty titles of published and forthcoming books and magazines.

St. Herman of Alaska Brotherhood
10 Beegum Gorge Road
P. O. Box 70
Platina, CA 96076

Typeset in Adobe Garamond.

Color separation for cover by Summerfield Graphics,
Santa Rosa, California.

Printed at Thomson-Shore, Inc., Dexter Michigan.